Palgrave Macmillan Studies in Banking and Financial Institutions

Series Editor
Philip Molyneux
University of Sharjah
Sharjah, United Arab Emirates

The Palgrave Macmillan Studies in Banking and Financial Institutions series is international in orientation and includes studies of banking systems in particular countries or regions as well as contemporary themes such as Islamic Banking, Financial Exclusion, Mergers and Acquisitions, Risk Management, and IT in Banking. The books focus on research and practice and include up to date and innovative studies that cover issues which impact banking systems globally.

More information about this series at
http://www.palgrave.com/gp/series/14678

Alessandra Tanda • Cristiana-Maria Schena

FinTech, BigTech and Banks

Digitalisation and Its Impact on Banking Business Models

Alessandra Tanda
Department of Economics and
Management
University of Pavia
Pavia, Italy

Cristiana-Maria Schena
Department of Economics
University of Insubria
Varese, Italy

ISSN 2523-336X   ISSN 2523-3378 (electronic)
Palgrave Macmillan Studies in Banking and Financial Institutions
ISBN 978-3-030-22425-7   ISBN 978-3-030-22426-4 (eBook)
https://doi.org/10.1007/978-3-030-22426-4

Cover illustration: TimeStopper / GettyImages
Cover design by eStudio Calamar

This Palgrave Pivot imprint is published by the registered company Springer Nature Switzerland AG
The registered company address is: Gewerbestrasse 11, 6330 Cham, Switzerland

CONTENTS

About the Authors

Alessandra Tanda is Assistant Professor of Banking and Finance at the Department of Economics and Management at the University of Pavia. She obtained her Ph.D. in Financial Markets and Institutions from Cattolica University of Milan. Her primary research interests include FinTech, banking corporate governance and corporate financial structure.

Cristiana-Maria Schena is Full Professor of Financial Institutions at the Department of Economics, University of Insubria since 2006. She is Director of CreaRes (Research Center for Ethics in Business and Social Responsibility) and Head of the course in "Finance, Markets and Financial Intermediaries" within the master course in "Economics, Laws and Corporate Finance". She has published widely, including on FinTech, governance, organisation and management of financial intermediaries, ethics in finance, social responsibility and non-financial reporting.

LIST OF TABLES

CHAPTER 1

Introducing the FinTech Revolution

Abstract The digitalisation of financial markets is having a profound impact on the nature of client financial product and service provision. New entrants (FinTech and BigTech firms) are now operating on the financial markets by leveraging advanced technologies and innovative business models, applying competitive pressure to incumbent firms. This book analyses the business models used by FinTech and BigTech firms and banking institutions in order to highlight differences and analogies, including in the light of current debates over the need for a renewed regulatory framework which balances the potential risks and opportunities generated by FinTech.

Keywords FinTech • BigTech • Digitalisation • Banks • Business model

1.1 The Digital Economy and Financial Services

The development of the digital economy is affecting all industries and business sectors and producing changes at an unprecedented speed and intensity (Arner et al. 2016). A new way of living, thinking and acting is emerging which is also impacting on people's economic lives: their spending habits and professional activities. Digitalisation simplifies life and changes our approach to services (OECD 2017). Its impact on the

© The Author(s) 2019
A. Tanda, C.-M. Schena, *FinTech, BigTech and Banks*, Palgrave Macmillan Studies in Banking and Financial Institutions,
https://doi.org/10.1007/978-3-030-22426-4_1

1

financial industry, and banking services in particular, is especially significant (Arner et al. 2016; Zetzsche et al. 2017) where new entrants are present: the so-called FinTech companies. These firms employ technological and digital solutions to provide financial services and are developing multiple innovative strategic approaches and business models that meet customers' interest and preferences.

As a consequence, the perimeter of the financial system is widening to include a new industry sector—FinTech. The financial market landscape has changed substantially, and technological innovation has eroded the boundaries between financial products and services and the subjects either authorised to provide them or actually providing them (EBA 2017). An additional result of this is that new competitive forces and dynamics are developing with consequences for the market share of incumbent financial intermediaries. The FinTech revolution is affecting banks in particular, which are having to rethink their business in the face of competition.

The main purpose of this work is to analyse the strategic choices adopted by the different types of operators (FinTech, BigTech and incumbent firms) in delivering banking services and examine the way digitalisation is affecting the business models employed by banks and other banking services providers. To this end, and to provide recent evidence on actual market development, we primarily consider Europe and compare it to other relevant international experiences (such as the USA and China), including as regards non-European companies entering the European market through a variety of organisational approaches and business models.

This analysis allows the opportunities and risks related to the various business models to be highlighted, in line with the Financial Stability Board (FSB 2017) and European Banking Authority (EBA 2018) suggestions. In addition, the work highlights the changes to the financial system structure currently underway globally. To this end, we employ a proprietary database that aggregates information on a large international sample, derived from various sources.

1.2   The Structure of the Book

The book is structured to highlight the distinctive features of FinTech, BigTech and incumbent operators and present an up-to-date view of the regulatory framework, above all at the European level. Chapter 2 clarifies the differences between the various types of new financial operators (FinTech, TechFin and BigTech), having excluded Tech companies operating as providers of technological solutions for financial intermediaries.

Once again in Chap. 2 we analyse the financial activities developed by FinTech and TechFin companies, stressing the peculiarities of their business model as compared to incumbent banks. In this part of the study, the discussion begins with an analysis of a representative FinTech sample operating in the European market.

This analysis is further developed in Chap. 3, taking into consideration a representative sample of BigTech companies (four US and two Chinese) which have employed a wide range of approaches to develop their financial market presence. In so doing, we have highlighted the differences between FinTech companies and their potential competitive strengths as compared to incumbent firms. Subsequently, we analyse the strategies adopted to date by the banks, both large and small and with different operational characteristics, to examine how they are grasping the opportunities offered by technological development and the digitalisation of business (Chap. 4). More specifically, in this part of the research we consider three main categories of banks, to highlight the specific characteristics of the strategic approaches adopted by

(a) the main international banks which are reacting proactively to the diverse demands emerging from their customers, including in response to competitive pressure from FinTech and BigTech companies. The case studies analysed (32 international banks particularly active in digitalisation terms) show that some international banks are actually leading or contributing significantly to innovation in some specific areas and provide evidence on the similarities and differences between European and other international non-European banks;

(b) small banks, underlining the possible strategic choices that can be adopted and citing the experience of small banks in some markets;

(c) the digital native banks, finally, to discuss how they differ from incumbents. In this case, too, our analysis is based on a proprietary dataset that integrates several sources and includes 22 digital banks. We have examined independent banks and those acting as part of banking groups or BigTech conglomerates, to highlight the differences in the strategic approaches adopted.

Overall, our evidence underlines the presence of multiple strategic approaches, as well as the distinctive features, strengths and weaknesses of each type of financial operator (both native digital institutions and incumbent firms).

Chapter 5 addresses some regulatory issues with reference to the scope of regulation and the boundaries of the FinTech activities. The initial regulatory "wait-and-see" approach was determined internationally by the belief that hasty regulatory intervention risked undermining the benefits of innovation. Lately, regulators have started to take more coordinated action, for the purposes of limiting the risks and closing the regulatory arbitrage gap. Uncontrolled activities by unregulated companies in financial markets constitute a significant threat in customer and investor protection, financial stability and financial market resilience terms. This chapter emphasises recent European regulatory initiatives.

Finally, Chap. 6 concludes with considerations on the future development of the banking and financial system and provides food for thought for policy takers and policy makers. The study's results contribute to the next-generation banking business model debate that has recently been the subject of the Bank for International Settlements-Basel Committee on Banking Supervision (hereafter BIS-BCBS) (2018) theoretical analysis.

In detail, our analysis shows that several business models co-exist in the banking industry. While FinTech and BigTech firms offer new and highly digitalised financial services, meeting consumers' demand and preferences, incumbent firms are reacting to various extents. Large banks are digitalising with varying degrees of commitment and innovation. Strategies vary, but mainly relate to shareholding, in-house development and partnership with FinTech and BigTech firms. The number of initiatives notwithstanding, most focuses on channel digitalisation, while only a few are pursuing true "digital disruption". On the other hand, smaller banks are apparently struggling to enact significant strategy and business model changes consistent with technological development. The survival of these smaller financial institutions may lie in partnerships with FinTech firms. Finally, the new business models proposed by native digital banks are also affecting the way banking and financial services are offered, contributing to changes in customer expectations.

Overall, the book shows that sluggish development and the difficulties encountered by banks play a role in the development of the new digital operators who often also benefit from a lighter regulatory framework than incumbent firms. A further relevant issue is the data processing and regulatory framework of new digital operators, which poses interesting client protection questions, to which the international legislation response is still fragmented and non-homogeneous.

REFERENCES

Arner, D. W., Barberis, J., & Buckley, R. P. (2016). The evolution of FinTech: New post-crisis paradigm. *Georgetown Journal of International Law, 47*(4), 1271–1320.

BIS-BCBS. (2018, February). *Sound practices. Implications of fintech developments for banks and bank supervisors.* Basel Committee on Banking Supervision—BIS. Retrieved March 27, 2019, from https://www.bis.org/bcbs/publ/d431.pdf.

EBA. (2017, August 4). *Discussion paper on the EBA's approach to financial technology (FinTech).* EBA/DP/2017/02.

EBA. (2018, July 3). *EBA report on the impact of Fintech on incumbent credit institutions' business models.*

FSB. (2017, June 27). *Financial stability implications from FinTech, supervisory and regulatory issues that merit authorities' attention.*

OECD. (2017). *Key-issues for digital transformation in the G20.*

Zetzsche, D. A., Buckley, R. P., Arner, D. W., & Barberis, J. N. (2017). *From FinTech to TechFin: The regulatory challenges of data-driven finance.* EBI working paper series, no. 6.

CHAPTER 2

FinTech Activities and Business Models: Analogies and Differences with the Traditional Financial Channels

Abstract Technological progress and the dissemination of innovation have enabled FinTech companies to emerge. These are currently able to offer products and services in all areas of traditional financial intermediation, often outside the regulatory perimeter. Not only do FinTech companies provide new products and processes, but they also enter the market with new business models and services which respond better to customers' demands and preferences. Via the unbundling and rebundling of financial services, FinTech companies are able to specialise in various business segments and potentially disrupt traditional incumbent activities. Nevertheless, in contrast to BigTech, FinTech companies have to collect and gather information and reach critical masses if they are to become formidable competitors.

Keywords FinTech • Unbundling • Business model • Financial services

2.1 Defining FinTech

To begin with, we must clarify that the definition of FinTech (Financial Technology) used in this book is limited to companies operating in financial intermediation mainly through technological or digital solutions (Schena et al. 2018).[1] More specifically, this includes both FinTech

© The Author(s) 2019   7
A. Tanda, C.-M. Schena, *FinTech, BigTech and Banks*, Palgrave
Macmillan Studies in Banking and Financial Institutions,
https://doi.org/10.1007/978-3-030-22426-4_2

companies set up to offer financial services and TechFin companies which started operations in other industries (mainly pre-existing technology and e-commerce) and only later began developing and distributing financial services (Zetzsche et al. 2017). In this book, TechFin thus includes BigTech companies, that is, companies that have departed from their original core business to develop financial services and products within their diversification strategies, including US Google, Apple, Facebook and Amazon (GAFA), Chinese Baidu, Alibaba and Tencent (BAT) and Japanese Sony and AEON.

What these FinTech and TechFin firms have in common is that they are all digital native companies using technology to develop innovative financial services. This is performed through applications or digital platforms (including open API (Application Programming Interface), electronic platforms or digital marketplaces) that facilitate contact with customers and fulfil their needs promptly with instant access services.

A first distinctive feature of FinTech development is "digital proximity". This radically modifies the nature of the firm-client relationship and disrupts incumbent firms' physical proximity advantage, replacing it with financial service user friendliness. More generally, technology allows geographical boundaries to be broken down and cross-border business to take place, information to circulate and be updated in a faster and cheaper way, relations with customers to be changed and financial transactions to be channelled through technological applications and digital platforms.

This provides an insight into the ways in which the new digital operators become more competitive, the more advanced the supporting infrastructure is (the internet, digital networks, big data, digital security, etc.), but also the higher the skills and capabilities related to research, elaboration, storage and secure transmission of information (big data analytics, machine learning, artificial intelligence, cloud-computing, DLT (Distributed Ledger Technology), etc.) become.[2]

Consequently, for the new financial operators, too, the growth and availability of resources for technological investment is key to development. Observing current market conditions shows that many FinTechs rely on rather simple technologies for their activities, while TechFin and, especially, BigTech firms already have highly sophisticated and advanced technological infrastructures (big data, artificial intelligence, etc.) (CB Insights 2017). A further aspect that can throw light on the differences is the diverse "origins" of these companies, implying diverse availability of data and information.

FinTech firms are start-ups specialised in a given financial sector and have to acquire information on customers to offer services. Additionally, they have to build their reputations to obtain operational credibility. Given their need for time to consolidate their databases, during the start-up phase, FinTech companies can struggle in comparison to incumbent firms. The latter, in fact, enjoy a large and consolidated client data asset.

Vice versa, BigTech, or more generally TechFin, firms can leverage previously acquired client trust and exploit their large data assets (big data), built up whilst developing pre-existing business, to offer their customers financial services, too (Arner et al. 2016; Zetzsche et al. 2017). BigTech firms acquire free information on the spending habits and payment methods of their numerous customers. This vast amount of information feeds the algorithms that automatically elaborate information and provide suggestions and proposals to subscribe to other services (including financial services) to these same customers. In so doing, BigTechs can satisfy customers' needs in a prompt and effective way, responding to their requests or anticipating their financial needs to foster spending capacity. This makes BigTech's powerful competitive advantage evident: this advantage is a major threat to incumbent firms which is larger and more worrying than FinTech's.

In the context of digitalisation, the strategic development factor is the availability and effective use of data and information on customers.[3] On the basis of these considerations, BigTech firms are described as "digital disruptors" within a still evolving financial system. This issue is especially relevant in the light of the fact that "the financial industry is one of the most data-oriented businesses" and that big data, collected and elaborated by BigTech firms through their global platforms "can be seen as a new type of asset, in terms of a profit source, instead of traditional fixed assets such as branches" (Nakaso 2017).

This might imply that incumbent displacement might be all the more rapid and intense the more FinTechs are able to employ technological solutions capable of meeting clients' financial needs and acquire and elaborate the relevant information effectively, to the extent of big data, in a similar way to BigTech firms. This may allow the soft information[4] that is at the basis of the peculiar role traditionally performed by banks and other regulated financial intermediaries to be replaced.[5] Nevertheless, at present, the new entry threat is already credible and pervasive. The competitive pressure may further increase as the number of FinTech companies increases, leading to rapid growth in operating volumes and increasing diversification in the financial services offered by these companies.

Additionally, the FinTech development dynamic is generating changes in the way customers behave. Users appreciate the capacity of these companies to provide fast, accessible and easy-to-use solutions for their financial needs. The capacity of new digital entrants to accord clients central importance as against products/service is determining progressive growth of trust in FinTech companies, especially among the youngest and most digitalised client groups (Capgemini-EFMA 2017). This competitive advantage is even more pronounced where BigTechs are concerned, in relation to their ability to personalise services, thus improving customer experience[6] (Sperimborgo 2016). This aspect is all the more important because customers' needs and preferences have changed over the years: as the European Banking Authority (EBA 2018) has highlighted, speed, attention to clients and flexibility have become key elements for customers choosing their financial products and financial services providers.[7]

Last but not least, a consideration of the distinctive features of new financial operators involves taking into account the processes underlying the supply of financial products. As will be examined in greater depth later in this book, FinTech is based on the unbundling[8] of financial services, that is, on the breakdown of production processes resulting in specialised products being offered via the creation of direct financial circuits (digital platforms) and other technological solutions (e.g. apps).

On one hand, this allows customers to perform financial transactions directly without having to rely on regulated financial intermediaries or financial markets. On the other, this type of business model means FinTech firms are not exposed to the risks implied by the financial services offered and can exploit operating areas that are not subject to regulatory provisions. This means that FinTech is commonly perceived as being able to offer "banking without the bank"[9] and as capable of displacing incumbents in shared business areas.

This approach is completely different from the universal or multibusiness model traditionally used by banks (also through the creation of complex groups) to satisfy the various client financial needs in an integrated manner. The adoption of this model implies a different type of risk management than that offered by the banks which are, also, subject to much heavier and more complex regulation burdens than FinTech companies. To throw more light on these issues, the following sections will elaborate on the areas of activities and business models used by FinTech companies, with the assistance of some examples.

2.2 Areas of Activity and Distinctive Features

The taxonomy of the financial activities carried out by FinTech is now diversified and capable of responding to an extremely wide range of clients' financial demands (Table 2.1). This can be detected by reference not only to the areas of original and most intense development (USA, UK[10] and China) but also in other countries in which FinTech constitutes a more recent phenomenon and one which is more limited in terms of operational volume and market share terms[11] (see EBA 2017). As an example, a recent research performed on a significant sample of FinTech firms working in Italy (with Italian and European headquarters) highlighted that the perimeter of the financial sector has widened significantly, thanks to the emergence of new operators variously specialised and active overall across the whole range of financial intermediation activities shown in Table 2.1.

A proprietary database relating to the sample analysed in an earlier study[12] has been appropriately updated and supplemented to take account of more recent Italian evolutions and international dynamics. This enables the business model used by FinTechs to be illustrated, highlighting its product and process specifics which show certain differences as compared to the financial activities performed by incumbent firms.

To begin with, it is important to specify that the activities carried out by FinTech firms internationally tend to be similar, operationally speaking, with the exception of the existence of conditions (limiting or more permissive) prompted by the various legal frameworks[13] and/or differing degrees of dissemination and accessibility of financial services[14] which impact on FinTech development and the types of services offered in the individual markets.

The principal objective of this volume is to highlight the business models of the various types of players active in the banking context, above all in the European context. For this reason, we will now analyse FinTech's activities, concentrating on the areas typically falling within the banking sphere and leaving insurance to one side whilst being aware of the important InsurTech developments taking place internationally.[15] We will also not examine the legal framework differences to be found in various countries.

Table 2.1 FinTech firms' financial intermediation activities

(a) Financing solutions

Equity-based financing			Debt financing (loans and debt securities placement)			
Pure equity crowdfunding (retail)	Club deals (identified investors; private placement targeting business angels for example)	Funding from institutional and/or qualified investors	Lending crowdfunding (or social lending) and P2P lending	Short-term funding: • Invoice lending; • Commercial credit	Club deals (identified investors; private placement targeting business angels for example)	Funding from institutional and/or qualified investor

(b) Investment services and activities

Trading	Financial management	Financial advice
Trading for retail and institutional clients: • trading platforms on listed and unlisted securities; • trading platforms on alternative assets (crypto currencies); • platforms on which to submit and carry out orders; • platforms enabling other traders' strategies to be emulated	Fund management service: aggregation of expenses performed with various payment tools (current accounts, credit cards, etc.) and monetary exit planning Electronic piggy bank: • setting aside of sums of money only; • setting aside of sums of money and investing in financial products	Traditional financial advice or with the support of advanced analysis tools (robo advisors) on third-party or own brand financial products

(c) Payment services

Money transfers		Payment solutions	
Fiat money (paper/legal)	Virtual money (crypto currencies)	Fiat money (paper/legal)	Virtual money (crypto currencies)

(d) Insurance services (InsurTech)

Insurance and pension services and products

2.2.1   *Financing Solutions*

In the provision of financing solutions, FinTechs take advantage of digital platforms constituting direct funding circuits (the digital marketplace) which users can access as borrowers or lenders. Borrowers are individuals or small firms (SMEs) interested in sourcing financial resources via equity or debts (bonds and more frequently loans).

In the debt securities resource area, individual FinTech firms offer solutions which respond to diverse specific client demands.[16] In particular, lending crowdfunding (or social lending) platforms, peer-to-peer (P2P) lending, are supplemented by FinTech firms offering short-term lending solutions, namely, invoice lending and commercial credit. In this latter, solutions are diversified and can encompass invoice lending, factoring and commercial credit circuits.

This variety of financial needs can be satisfied via various types of lenders. Platforms target retail investors in particular, and in such cases pure crowdfunding can be identified. Alternatively, financial resources can be supplied by investors which the platforms select on the basis of criteria which vary according to the platforms considered.[17] These are club deals, that is, they take place via private placement targeting specifically identified subjects (e.g. business angels). A further possibility is the intervention of professional or authorised investors (such as investment funds, insurance firms, etc.) which can underwrite shares (bonds and equities) when they are issued or buy them from FinTechs in the event that the latter have already co-funded the issue.

These partnerships between FinTech and financial intermediaries are especially interesting and can foster the development of activities. In fact, the presence of institutional investors in an equity or lending crowdfunding campaign can contribute to making a digital marketplace more transparent and efficient. The institutional investors can, in fact, contribute to improving the reputation and credibility of a FinTech firm in that their participation in a primary market deal offers retail investors indications of the quality of the platform and/or investment project. These same institutional investors can also offer liquidity services on secondary markets of equities or debt securities placed by means of FinTech platforms in the event that these commit to absorbing demands from the FinTech company's clientele in the sale of underwritten securities subsequent to placement.

Vice versa, in the absence of professional and qualified investors, the market hosted by the FinTech firm can turn out to be strongly illiquid and risky, in addition to opaque, in consideration of the frequently limited information regarding both the selection criteria used for borrowing firms on the platform and the methods by which a risk class is attributed to these.

To this, it should be added that the various business models adopted by individual FinTech firms can impact significantly on the incentives for correct behaviour as regards platforms' users and, above all, by lenders.

As previously highlighted, FinTech firms usually limit their activities to making a "place for such trading" (a marketplace) available to users which constitutes a direct alternative to the traditional channels managed by regulated financial intermediaries. As alternative FinTech firms can co-fund the projects they offer on their platforms (issuing a part of the funding or underwriting part of the equity or bond issue) thus sharing the risk with other investors. In such cases, FinTech companies can choose whether to remain exposed to counterparty or credit risk, sell securities on to third-party investors or proceed to securitisation operations.

With special reference to lending crowdfunding, studies carried out on the business models adopted by FinTech companies internationally (Kirby and Worner 2014; FSB 2018) highlight three main approaches:

- A client segregated account model: platforms which simply match up lenders and borrowers (matching platforms). Contracts are drawn up between the two parties and the funds transit outside the platform via an external payment account. In such cases, platforms simply showcase and connect up subjects wanting to invest and those needing to source funds.
- A notary model: similar to the previous type but the funds are collected by a bank tasked with this. The bank issues the loan to the platform's client when the sum required has been reached. The original investors receive the equivalent of a credit note from the platform ("notarised" matching platforms).
- A "guaranteed" return model: in this model (frequently used in China and less common in Europe), the platform collects the funds from its own clients and pays them on the basis of the debtor's risk class. In such cases, it is the platform itself which issues the loan but in some cases, the funds are issued by hedge funds or banks (balance sheet lenders).

Clearly, with the guaranteed return model, investors obtain returns from the platform in return for the funds issued and do not take on the credit risk as regards the borrowers who are funded directly by the platform. This latter thus collects funds and lends, exposing itself to the risk of debtor insolvency, while clients lending money are exposed to the risk of platform insolvency. Where loans are issued by hedge funds or banks, the situation created is one in which the credit risk falls on financial intermediaries rather than the platform.

In the other two business models, on the other hand, the platform simply links up borrowers and lenders and the credit risk falls entirely on the lenders. In particular, in the former case (client segregated) the platform accords risk classes on the basis of which it "matches" borrowers and lenders. The loan contract is drawn up directly by the two parties.

In the latter case (notary), the platform issues a credit note which is frequently considered a security and thus transfers the credit risk from the bank issuing the loan to the platform's clients who sign up to the deal and transfer funds to the lending bank (Kirby and Worner 2014).

Note, furthermore, that the development of securitisation operations performed by P2P lending and lending crowdfunding platforms can increase the risk of moral hazard and reduced attention to the quality of the loan by the platforms themselves, similar to that highlighted in the past in the area of lending activities in the event of the application of the "originate to distribute" model.[18]

It is important to underline that, in the event that the financial mediation, underwriting, negotiation and lending services cited thus far are offered by financial intermediaries (investment firms in the form of brokers or dealers; banks; other lending institutions; consumer lending companies; factoring firms; etc.) and/or regulated primary and secondary financial markets, the law requires specific conduct and management rules safeguarding clients and the integrity of the financial system.

By contrast, the requirements for equity and lending crowdfunding platforms vary considerably from country to country and are frequently not regulated at all. It is only in some cases, and for some types of business model, that they are subject to similar or equivalent regulations to those required of intermediaries and regulated financial markets or specific rules issued in consideration of the fact that simply extending the norms currently in force is not sufficient to cover the innovative business practices adopted by FinTech companies for its financial services.[19]

The unbundling of the productive processes which is the result of operational specialisation decisions can thus enable FinTech firms to position themselves in operational segments which escape regulatory requirements as well as those market spaces in which financial intermediaries do not succeed in formulating effective responses to client demands. In fact, the FinTech firms primarily target the mass market, succeeding in rapidly increasing the volume of their activities on the basis of extremely straightforward products, relatively uncontrolled by traditional financial intermediaries, such as invoice trading and funding SMEs more generally. Embryonic at the European level this phenomenon[20] is already present in the USA where FinTech companies succeed in working without regulatory controls and significantly filling the "gap" left in banking loan provision to small and medium-sized firms.[21]

Of the principal American FinTech companies whose strategic objective is to fund underbanked subjects (and above all SMEs) PayPal stands out[22] as having reached in 2018 operational volumes positioning it in the top five US lenders (alongside Wells Fargo, Bank of America and JP Morgan Chase). In particular, PayPal has underlined that, in contrast to those of the banks, its lending activities consist substantially of a huge number of extremely small loans to SMEs. Furthermore, for the purposes of credit risk evaluation, rather than adopting credit scoring techniques applied by the banks, PayPal uses algorithms which analyse the development prospects of the firm applying for a loan on the basis of data relating to the sale of goods and services which it performs over time on its digital platform (merchant). Moreover, PayPal uses a loan payback mechanism based on automatic deductions of a share of each sale which the merchant carries out on its platform (Rooney 2018).

Today the operational dimensions of the FinTech firms working in the international and European lending markets and, to an even greater extent, in the equity market are still relatively limited as compared to the volume of business managed internationally by incumbent firms. This has, to date, led the supranational bodies to hold that FinTech generates no specific stability risk on a systemic level (FSB 2018). However, these same regulatory bodies consider it important to monitor this marketplace, including for the purposes of giving further consideration to regulation methods. We consider this approach to be valid for various reasons.

A first aspect is macro-economic in nature and emerges from an awareness that the development of direct retail circuits not subject to conduct rules can generate a non-optimal allocation of savings and the financial resources available within the economic system. The platform can effectively select subjects and firms which cannot access bank loans because they are significantly in debt or, more generally, uncreditworthy. This is made even more plausible in the somewhat commonplace cases in which FinTechs operate as marketplaces alone as a result of lower incentives to appropriate screening which could derive from a consideration that the risk deriving from transactions carried out within the equity or lending crowdfunding activity fall purely on the lenders/investors, typically retail, and not on the platform itself.

A second and equally important element relates to customers. An analysis of the different business models underlines that the digital marketplace offered by FinTech firms, similar to all other direct, unregulated circuits, raises investor protection questions as regards retail clients (investors and lenders) and, more generally speaking, clients without the necessary financial skills.[23]

We would argue that the importance of this theme emerges forcefully from an analysis of the numerous and frequent cases of FinTech platform bankruptcy and difficulty (due to inappropriate market practices, mistaken borrower creditworthiness estimates and fraud) which have generated considerable repercussions on clients (Arner et al. 2016; ASIC 2017; BIS-FSB 2017; Financial Times 2018); and the Chinese example is especially revealing in this respect (World Bank Group and the People's Bank of China 2018), in particular as regards the powerfully negative effect generated on retail clients.[24]

With specific reference to the European context, it should be highlighted that the regulatory framework is changing and further changes will take place in the competitive dynamics between financial operators and in their business model choices. In fact, in the context of the Capital Market Union Action Plan and in a belief in the benefits of convergence in the rules governing platforms in Europe, the European Commission (2018) has recently submitted a European Crowdfunding Service Providers (ECSPs) regulation proposal to the European Parliament.[25] If it is approved, this regulation will, on one hand, allow equity and lending crowdfunding platforms operating to the benefit of European firms to enjoy mutual recognition within the European Union (EU) and, on the other, subject them to supervision.

2.2.2   Investment Services and Activities

Many FinTech firms have developed products and apps linked to investment services and some of these are innovative as compared to those offered by incumbent firms. As Table 2.1 highlights, individual platforms can operate in three distinct areas namely trading, financial management and financial advice services. In each of these segments, whilst adopting unbundling techniques, FinTechs tend to combine similar services.

Trading services are offered by individual platforms to retail investors or institutional investors. Some FinTechs offer clients the chance not only to negotiate but also to copy other traders' strategies (copy trading) in a digital environment which combines classic trading functions (buying and selling securities) with social aspects (community creation and the chance to discuss and share experiences with other traders via a blog on the site).

The financial management services offered by FinTech firms, on the other hand, generally target retail investors enabling them to view what they have spent with their various credit or debit cards in a single virtual environment as well as formulating savings or personalised expense plans. Electronic piggy bank services are a further financial management service, enabling people to set aside even very small sums of money periodically in a virtual wallet.

A first type of electronic piggy bank enables clients to save a certain amount of money with which to buy goods and services. Once they have achieved their targets, users are notified and can, if they like, purchase the desired goods or services. However, access to the money set aside over time is in no way limited and thus clients can use all or part of it at any time even before reaching their targets.

A second type of electronic piggy bank, on the other hand, allows an investment function to be linked to the savings app. In this way, FinTech firms offer a similar service to savings plans. In this case, the money accumulated can be invested in financial instruments or investment funds selected by the FinTech app. Specifically, individual FinTech firms draw up catalogues which can include their own or third-party products (such as securities and investment funds). In this latter case, clients use a bank or other financial intermediary to carry out purchases of products chosen from FinTech catalogues.

With reference to financial advice services it should, first and foremost, be noted that these are a peculiar area of development of FinTech firms which use automatised procedures to formulate investment proposals (robo advice) which primarily target retail investors.[26] In particular, clients' demographic and wealth data are processed via algorithms enabling personalised investment proposals to be generated in very short time frames. These can offer FinTech firms' own products (such as investment funds) or third-party products (sometimes offered on the basis of partnership agreements). This latter case generally involves investors making the investments advised them by the FinTech firm via an intermediary authorised to receive and implement financial tool orders.

Also in reference to investment services, it is important to note that where trading services, savings management and financial advice services are offered by incumbent firms, these latter are subject to supervisory laws designed to safeguard clients and limit conflicts of interest, though not in a uniform way internationally. Fintech firms, instead, thanks to the unbundling of products and non-direct implementation of all the services necessary to the development of investment services, by contrast, might exploit spaces not subject to specific regulations. For this reason, even for the investment services, investor safeguards constitute an aspect worthy of attention in the event that FinTech firms do not function as supervised financial intermediaries and thus are not obliged to full and overall respect for the legal framework as regards appropriate client profiling (the Markets in Financial Instruments Directive II (or MiFID II) in the EU) and transparency and pre-contractual and contractual fairness regulations.[27] This is an extremely delicate matter in which artificial intelligence algorithms are used (Barbagallo 2018), in reference to which—in the absence of regulatory supervision—we cannot know whether these take sufficient account of investor's risk propensity and effective financial needs.[28]

Within this framework clients' self-protection is paramount. Clients are free to express their preferences on if and where to invest, paying attention to verifying a series of aspects: whether a FinTech firm is subject to some form of control; the truthfulness of the information supplied; any conflicts of interest in its activities or on the basis of criteria which are not coherent with their risk propensities and effective investment needs. At the same time it should be underlined that, in this financial intermediation environment, too, FinTech firms are exerting strong innovation pressures. This is highlighted by the development of algorithm-driven financial planning services based on the application of artificial intelligence to investment services. This effectively enables huge quantities of big data to be stored and processed in real time, determining a platform self-earning process which enables optimal market interpretation and new investments or the rebalancing of existing portfolios to be proposed.

Lastly, it is important to underline that a further service being disseminated thanks to the development of digitalisation is the robot-for-advice service. In contrast to the services considered thus far, this does not target the end investor but rather the financial consultant who can thus use avant-garde technological solutions to support the financial advice services offered to clients. A great many firms are now taking advantage of this worldwide, both FinTech and incumbent firms.

This allows us to highlight that, in the wealth management context, too, a plurality of digital business models are developing (Wealth Tech) which are not exclusively automatised but also hybrid, namely models in which technology helps to improve customer experience and develop increasingly sophisticated and multivariable segmentation approaches (Di Mascio 2018).

2.2.3   Payment Services

Money transfer services (fiat money and virtual currency) and payment solutions (via fiat money or virtual currency) is the area in which FinTech first developed globally and in which, precisely for this reason, an especially large number of operators is capable of supplying advanced and efficient services. In particular, the money transfer services offered by FinTech firms enable them to operate across borders very rapidly and with especially low costs even without bank accounts. In fact, certain operational solutions enable cash to be used to top up a prepaid card or virtual wallet, even at specific physical retail outlets or automated teller machines (ATMs).[29]

A high number of advanced payment solutions in technological terms are available such as apps linked to current accounts, credit cards and virtual wallets—detached from current accounts—which can be activated and accessed *via* a range of devices (smartphones and tablets) and topped up with legal or virtual currency.

Wallets differ from current accounts primarily in their purpose. Current accounts are fundamentally deposit contracts for liquidity purposes to which payments tools are attached. Wallets, on the other hand, are mainly payment tools. The subject offering the service also differs. Virtual wallets are not necessarily set up by banks (or other supervised intermediaries). This is certainly the case, for example, of crypto currency wallets (not currently considered legal tender) which are set up exclusively by unregulated and unsupervised firms. This has legal implications: where banks fail, clients with current accounts are protected by guarantees on sums up to a maximum which is legally fixed (100,000 euros in the European context); where unregulated wallet suppliers fail, there are no safeguards on the sums deposited.[30]

In certain cases, payment services are equipped with avant-garde security and identity verification tools including facial recognition and digital fingerprinting in order to guarantee users a high level of transaction security.

One of the first FinTech operators to enter this financial market sector was American PayPal, set up in 1998 as a money transfer and digital payment transfer system via the internet and with technology which makes use of the existing payment infrastructure. Today, PayPal is one of the sector's most important operators internationally, operating in over 200 countries and offering its clientele a wide range of financial solutions. PayPal has achieved this on the basis of a development strategy formulated in-house and by creating a group made up of financial companies set up for the distribution of payment services which were subsequently supplemented with loan services (including revolving credit cards). As we have already highlighted, this operational diversification in the lending area has been made possible by PayPal's use of information acquired over time as an online payment manager.[31] PayPal is clear evidence of the competitive potential of the FinTech firms which can, over time, achieve significant size and market shares and diversify their services both independently and in partnership with technological firms operating in other sectors at the expense of incumbent firms.

Competition between financial operators would seem, moreover, likely to grow further in various directions. In reference to the European context it should, for example, be remembered that regulations on free cross-border circulation of data and information processing security (General Data Protection Regulation or GDPR) pose serious challenges to the banks in the implementation of technological tools serving to implement the client data protection required of them (EBA 2018).[32] Furthermore, the new Payment Services Directive (the so-called PSD2) has allowed third-party providers (TPPs) access to data relating to banking clients' current accounts on condition that current account holders give their assent. If, on one hand, this enables FinTech firms to use especially valuable information—previously held exclusively by the banks—free of charge, on the other hand this same EU directive sets out that only TPPs subject to authorities' supervision can make use of this opportunity (EBA 2018; Schena et al. 2018; Scopsi 2018). This may push Fintech companies in the direction of acquiring the licences required to operate in a regulated context (e.g. as payment institutions or electronic money institutions) unless they continue to base their activities on alternative client information from the soft information held by the banks.

In the context of payment services it should, lastly, be remembered that a considerable number of FinTech firms has specialised in managing virtual money (crypto currencies), enabling clients to move money in crypto currencies and withdraw cash (legal tender) at physical withdrawal points which access crypto currency wallets and to make payments at outlets directly in crypto currencies (mainly Bitcoin). In various countries, ATMs have recently been installed which enable clients to access crypto currencies in their electronic wallets and withdraw and deposit this at physical outlets. This has been possible in countries—including European countries—where crypto currencies, whilst not legal tender, have not been declared illegal.

It should be noted that specific rules on crypto currencies have only been drawn up in a few countries while other national authorities have adopted a "wait-and-see" approach.[33]

2.3   BUSINESS MODEL EVOLUTION

What we have seen thus far for the individual FinTech activity areas confirms the specific features of a business model essentially based on a combination of two elements: on one hand, a marked specialisation on a business line corresponding to the outcome of the unbundling of traditional financial products and, on the other, the creation of direct digital circuits which facilitate financial transactions, making services more accessible and the response to clients' financial demands more rapid allowing for progressive customer experience improvements.

The development of FinTech cannot be considered a "mere" distribution channel innovation levering digital proximity, however. As proof of this, we have highlighted the multiplicity of innovations relating to the production process and the range of financial products and services underlining the way in which technology plays an integral part in the operational processes and services offered.

As regards processes, FinTech's ability to shorten time frames and reduce service access costs should also be highlighted, based on the use of algorithms which process client data rapidly and formulate operational proposals. This enables FinTech firms to both offer traditional financial services in a more efficient way (e.g. lending and invoice lending where FinTech firms provide ultra-rapid responses to funding requests and cash is deposited in client current accounts in the space of a few days) and innovate their services, proposing mass market services (such as robo advice, a novelty for the finance sector).

As regards product innovations, the rapidly growing variety of new services as alternatives to traditional ones (electronic wallets, closed commercial circuits, copy trading, crypto currencies, etc.) is evident, enabling FinTech firms to respond in an increasingly variegated way to clients' financial needs.[34]

To fully understand this phenomenon, it is important to highlight that FinTech firms' development strategies evolve over time and gradually lead to the adoption of increasingly innovative and competitive business models. To clarify this, we will list here certain focal points which, we believe, should result in the phenomenon not being underestimated on the basis of hasty assessments based on the apparent "marginality" of these operators. It is, in fact, true that these digital natives take on the initial start-up phase with extremely limited activity volumes as compared to those of the traditional financial intermediation market, especially in consideration of the need for progressive development of client acquisition marketing techniques.

However, thanks also to the telematic dissemination of services and to client interest, this development has been rapid and significant. And it is not simply a matter of a few large-scale players, such as previously cited PayPal. The international data demonstrate that FinTech firm numbers are continuing to grow and in an especially significant way. Furthermore, most active FinTech firms have got past the start-up phase and activity growth volumes and market value witness the capacity of these firms to consolidate and develop.[35] It should be added that growth in size and operational evolution have led to some FinTech companies being listed on the stock exchange as shown by certain recent European operations.[36] Other operators have initiated aggregation and merger processes in order to pursue size growth objectives.[37]

This information is to be read together with that relating to FinTech's client segment of choice—retail. Taking into consideration, for example, the average sum involved in lending platform transactions, it is clear that the sums involved are generally especially small and have been dropping recently, internationally. This shows that FinTech's expansion is based on a more and more intense penetration of the retail segment (SMEs, professionals and individual borrowers as regards retail investors) to whom incumbent firms do not always offer adequate responses *via* consumer credit operations and banking transactions, especially in consideration of the onerous nature of their credit selection processes. Thus the FinTech market share, even when it is modest overall, reflects a growing number of deals and investors investing sums which are limited in size, if taken singly.[38]

Drawing on the multiplicity of individual cases in the European context, and at an international level, a tangible evolution in business strategies implemented by the main FinTech operators is visible.

In the first place, a progressive diversification in activities is visible on the strength of integrated service combinations. Of the many potential examples, we will cite the case of Oval Money which developed the electronic piggy bank services. The latter is offered also by other operators, but Oval Money has declared its intention of giving its own clients the chance to link an investment service to the piggy bank (https://www.ovalmoney.com).

In some cases, FinTech firms have decided to develop physical networks alongside digital networks or create group structures by acquiring other FinTech firms with different operational specialisation. An especially articulated example of this in operational and distributional solution terms is that of Borsa del Credito, an Italian lending platform[39] which is part of a company group (the holding firm is Business Innovation Lab S.p.a.) which encompasses other subsidiaries subject to regulation, namely Mo.Net S.p.a. (a payment institution which carries out P2P services for loans with instalment repayment) and ART SGR S.p.A.[40] In June 2018, Borsa del Credito announced the creation of a capillary physical network of agents across Italy and the development of new partnerships with Italian financial intermediaries. In July 2018, it signed a partnership with Mamacrowd (an equity crowdfunding platform) to diversify services offered to SMEs by a FinTech supply chain. In March 2019, it launched a loan designed ad hoc for Italian Amazon sellers operating on the e-commerce portal for at least three months.

Recourse to partnership agreements is increasingly commonplace and takes place not only between FinTech firms with different operational specialisations (such as that cited above between crowdfunding platforms) but also on the initiative of FinTech firms interested in working with other market operators (e.g. financial information elaboration firms, funds for credit guarantee established by national governments, credit mutual guarantee funds, etc.). This enables firms to consolidate operational development and offer increasingly complex and qualified financial services to their customers.

Of the many possible examples, we will cite Workinvoice,[41] which signed a partnership agreement with CRIBIS (CRIF group firm specialising in business information) in September 2018 for the development of the CRIBIS Cash service which integrates the commercial credit information developed by CRIBIS (530 million data points serving for the optimisation of analysis models used by investors operating on the marketplace) with the marketplace access developed by Workinvoice.

A further especially interesting example is the development trajectory followed by the FinTech firm October (previously Lendix), a French crowdlending firm for companies operating in various European countries including France, Spain, Italy and Belgium. Specifically, October supplied a total of 11.3 million euros in credit in 2018 (230 million since its inception) and generated over 230,000 loan contracts to firms. The funds come from over 15,000 private lenders and institutional investors. In Italy, October was the first lending platform for Italian SMEs to offer, from April 2018 onwards, the access to the guarantee fund set up by the Italian Ministry of Economic Development to its lenders (in the case of the default of the SME funded, the guarantee covers 40–80% of the residual capital). Furthermore, in May 2018, it signed a partnership agreement with an important credit mutual guarantee consortium (Confidi Systema!) which constitutes an important client pool.

Partnerships with financial intermediaries also constitute an important strategic approach used, to varying effect, by FinTech firms to develop their client services. In this context, an especially important part is played by partnerships which enable FinTech firms to respond more effectively to market segments which are not currently significantly covered by banks (especially the larger ones) such as SMEs which is of great significance in a large number of European countries.

The examples cited in this work have thrown light on the positive role which can be played by the joint presence of institutional investors (investment funds, alternative investment funds or AIFs, etc.) on crowdfunding platforms both in terms of the signals this sends out to retail investors and the increase in volume of financial resources made available to fund borrowers. In addition, the progressive increase in partnership agreements with financial intermediaries is worthy of note as these work alongside FinTech firms in their securitisation operations,[42] enabling the credit risk linked to their share in co-funding clients to be transferred to the market.

The vivacity of Fintech's strategic approaches also emerges clearly from the share acquisition policies in regulated financial intermediaries which some firms are undertaking to develop their activities under a regulatory umbrella or expand internationally. An example of the former has already been examined above, in reference to the case of the group which Borsa del Credito is part of. An example of international expansion is Moneyfarm, which began life in 2012 in Italy (where it is now a primary digital operator in the savings sector) before expanding in 2015 into the UK and, in 2018, into Germany via the acquisition of Vaamo, the German digital asset management pioneer and now one of the country's main robo advisors.[43]

Notes

1. Contrary to what has been done elsewhere, we exclude Tech firms from the FinTech category as these do not offer financial services but develop technological solutions that can be applied to the financial markets and hence develop product and services that are instrumental or functional to the financial intermediation process. On this, see Arner et al. (2016) and FSB (2017a).
2. Big data derives from the acquisition of a huge amount of detailed information generated and disseminated by a wide range of tools and sources including tracking information on websites, cookies, analysis of online consumer spending habits, social networks and so on. Analysis of this information is designed to assess social preferences, individual spending models and activities by companies.
3. The importance of data and the use of data in a digitalised "data-driven" economy have been described by Nakaso (2017): "*To describe how data utilization has evolved over years, I would like to use the example of maps. Over the years, many people have attempted to make maps as accurate as possible, which have provided us with remarkable benefits. Even today we enjoy the benefits of using geographical data, such as 'Google Maps'. However, what is different from the past is that we are no longer users of data only. Our access logs to these services themselves constitute a new set of big data, and potentially have their own value to be utilized. In today's society, data is a kind of resource, and power belongs to those who are able to collect and efficiently utilize such big data. It is analogous to the economic power of countries with large amounts of petroleum resources, which was increased after they enhanced their processing capacity and sales channels*".
4. On the differences between "hard" and "soft information" and their application to financial markets, see Liberti and Petersen (2018).
5. As has been well described by Gobbi (2016): "*The markets where banks are likely to suffer the most are those for services, where the production function is*

highly intensive in data processing such as payments, standardized consumer credit, brokerage of securities, and passively managed funds. If technology allows soft information to be sufficiently substituted with an effective analysis of big data, other markets, such as small and medium enterprises loans, could also be at risk".

6. Customer experience can be defined as clients' experiences during their interaction with the companies from which they acquire products and services.

7. Several analyses have underlined that BigTech firms have built a reputation that makes them appealing to a large share of consumers (Sperimborgo 2016; Barba Navaretti et al. 2017; OICV-IOSCO 2017), also as compared to incumbent firms (Baker et al. 2017; Jakšič and Marinc 2015). For instance, back in 2013, a survey by Viacom showed that the 75% of interviewees would consider buying financial products from big e-commerce platforms (Google, Amazon, etc.), rather than those offered by traditional financial intermediaries. Additionally, most users showed a marked aversion to bank visits, preferring a visit to the dentist (Viacom 2013).

8. Note that *"unbundling is a method to break down products and services into parts so only necessary parts can be provided according to need; for example, unbundling makes it possible to provide a limited scope of services, such as payments and loans, instead of providing all banking services including payments, deposits, loans, and asset management all together"* (Fujitsu 2018).

9. To the best of our knowledge, Worthington and Welch's paper (2010) was the first to cite this expression.

10. The UK, and London in particular, has always had a more innovation-focused financial market and one which is more similar in some ways to the powerfully market-oriented US experience. For this reason the UK has attracted a significant number of FinTech initiatives native to other countries. These FinTech firms were able to set up in the UK and, in the case of restricted activities, request licences from the British supervisory authorities and work in Europe on the basis of the mutual recognition principle. In the wake of the UK's decision to leave the European Union and with the prospect of a Brexit "no deal", certain firms have already got to work on guaranteeing continuity of service to their European clients, applying for the permits required in other countries. Of these, for example, Satispay obtained authorisation to work as a payment institution from the Luxembourg authorities in the first months of 2019 (Finextra 2019).

11. In the European context, Italian FinTech development has been delayed. In particular, FinTech investments are still limited as compared to other European countries such as the UK, Germany, France and the Netherlands (Banca d'Italia 2017; PWC 2018). The most recent estimates by PWC (PWC 2019) show that, as compared to a total of 216 billion dollars trans-

acted in the UK, Italy has registered transactions worth 38 billion dollars, a fifth of the UK figure, a third of the German total and half that of France. Despite this slow development, in Italy, too, expected growth rates are important in terms both of numbers of firms and revenues and transacted volumes.

12. See Schena et al. (2018), in which a sample of 71 FinTech companies operating in Italy in March 2018 was analysed in depth.

13. Think, for example, of the impact generated by different tax laws or planned regulation in the various countries.

14. Services accessible *via* apps and telematic links have acted as strategic levers to FinTech's development in Africa. Similarly, in China, FinTech's ultra-intense development has been accompanied by an increase in the spread of financial services and greater inclusion of segments of the population who previously did not use banks (Hau et al. 2017).

15. InsurTech identifies the insurance and pension services offered *via* innovative channels and using advanced technologies which enable the risks linked to insurance activities to be managed in interesting ways. On this matter see, amongst others, OECD (2018) and EIOPA (2017).

16. For further information, see CGFS-FSB (2017), Bofondi (2017), and Claessens et al. (2018).

17. Some of the criteria used to this end by FinTechs are the following: sufficient wealth, previous working experience in the finance sector and/or specialist educational profiles (economics graduates) or being part of a business angel network.

18. On risk translation phenomena between FinTech and regulated financial intermediaries (banks and institutional investors), see FSB (2017b), Appendix 6 ("Lending-based crowdfunding in the euro area: credit provision outside of the banking sector" contributed by Christian Weistroffer and Lieven Hermans at the ECB). Kirby and Worner (2014) had previously highlighted "*Interconnectedness through securitisation practices and bank involvement: there have been recent examples of the securitisation of peer-to-peer unsecured loans. This opens the market to new investment, but also opens the rest of the financial market to exposure to packaged loans which are predominately unsecured in nature. (…) Even subprime loans were partially backed by some form of collateral*".

19. See Chap. 5 for further considerations on the regulation theme.

20. With reference to the European context, see the analysis by ECB (2018). In the Italian national context, where the presence of SMEs is especially high, the demand for credit by such firms is still today much higher than banking system supply. The rapid development of the main FinTech operators, including Credimi (invoice trading operator subject to regulations) and Borsa del Credito (lending marketplace) testifies to the ability

of these firms to penetrate markets in which the banks have not succeeded in formulating an adequate response to the financial demands of SMEs.

21. As regards the US market the Federal Reserve Bank's 2017 report highlighted the fact that, whilst profitability is improving, SMEs find it difficult to access bank loans and, for this reason, are turning increasingly to online lenders not subject to regulation.

22. While PayPal has provided loans since its inception, we feel it is most appropriate to classify it as FinTech despite the fact that many studies classify it as BigTech, presumably because it is one of the largest players in the world and because, in 2002, it was bought up by eBay, the online auction and sale site. Subsequently PayPal was made independent of eBay in 2015, the year in which it was also listed on the US stock exchange NASDAQ.

23. Kirby and Worner (2014) report that "*Investors can and do make decisions based on personal biases and persuasive narrative, rather than on financial experience, due to the social networking aspect of peer-to-peer lending platforms. Neither government reviews nor the media have highlighted this point but it has been demonstrated substantially in academic work on the use of soft information, narrative, trust and pictures in peer-to-peer lending*".

24. As Claessens et al. have pointed out (2018) China has rapidly become the principal world market in P2P lending (followed by the USA and the UK) thanks to an initially very favourable legal framework. In 2016 new loans granted by Chinese FinTech platforms were equivalent to 40% of bank loans. However, cases of platform difficulty and default have been so numerous as to prompt regulatory intervention before the risks are transformed into market stability problems. The Chinese authorities intervened in 2016 and 2017, banning P2P lending platforms from gathering funds for themselves (i.e. with conflicts of interest), selling insurance policies unless they are authorised intermediaries and granting loans to students. Furthermore the laws regarding ultra-short term loans (cash loans) were made stricter. This has led to a significant contraction in the number and operational volume of Chinese lending platforms. Some platforms have closed down and others have been merged but not without generating especially negative effects on clients.

25. See Sect. 5.2.2 for a more in-depth examination of the European crowdfunding regulation proposals.

26. For a more in-depth examination of automatised financial advice and its implications in operational and regulatory terms, see Capgemini-EFMA (2017), Consob et al. (2017), Pia (2017), and ESAs (2018).

27. See Sect. 5.2.3 for an in-depth look at the robo advice regulatory regime in Europe.

28. On the various ways in which wealth management is defined (with or without human intervention) and the functioning of algorithms, see Di Mascio

(2018). On the more general theme of the opportunities and risks linked to the use of algorithms and artificial intelligence in the financial sector, see BaFin (2018) who also refers to previous studies on this theme carried out by the European Supervisory Authorities and the Financial Stability Board.

29. As an example, in several countries ATMs enabling clients to top up their Bitcoin wallets exist. Though supplied by a BigTech firm, an example is Amazon cash which enables a client's Amazon account (i.e. an electronic wallet expressed in legal tender usable exclusively on Amazon) to be topped up at certain partner outlets. *Via* cash deposits Amazon clients can transfer cash to this electronic wallet.

30. Quadriga, the main crypto currencies platform in Canada is an interesting case in point. In 2019, the sudden death of the portal's owner, the sole holder of the platform's access passwords and the only person who knew them, led to crypto currencies worth around 200 million dollars being frozen. Investors were denied access to their crypto currency wallets hosted by the platform (Forbes 2019).

31. PayPal currently leads a group listed on the stock exchange and made up of subsidiaries (Venmo and Xoom) which are authorised as money transmitters by the supervisory authorities with jurisdiction over the individual geographical areas in which they work. Furthermore, the PayPal Europe subsidiary is an authorised credit institution in Luxembourg and is supervised by Commission de Surveillance du Secteur Financier (CSSF). The group offers various web services including PayPal Cash, PayPal Credit (revolving credit), prepaid credit cards and payment and lending services for businesses (merchants).

32. With reference to the technology underlying certain innovative payment systems known as DLT and Blockchain, it is worth remembering that the European Commission constantly monitors the development of these technologies for potential application on financial markets, including in the context of transaction validation and safety. This same commission has created a European working group (EU Blockchain Observatory & Forum) which identifies trends and development initiatives in this technology, fostering European level information and know-how exchange on blockchain and formulating advice for policy makers (www.eublockchainforum.eu).

33. See Sect. 5.2.5 for a review of the principal legal initiatives on crypto currencies undertaken at the European and international levels.

34. Innovation is continuous over time. Think, for example, of the growing application of the crowdfunding model to the real estate sector, in which the funds gathered serve to buy real estate (new or for renovation) to earn money from or to sell on for capital gains purposes. Moreover, the specific features of the real estate market have implications which prompt consid-

eration of the risks for clients linked to the opaque nature and limited liquidity of the FinTech generated market.

35. PWC (2017) has estimated that over 18,400 FinTech firms exist globally and of these only 4000 were set up after 2012. Furthermore, in the payment sector alone over 1500 firms are involved, 369 on which have been set up over the last five years. This shows that the majority of these companies is no longer in the start-up phase and some are now extremely large and operate in multiple countries. As far as the market value of these firms is concerned, the mobile wallet segment alone is worth 2.4 billion dollars in investments while mobile-Point of Sale (or mobile-POS) is worth 2.2 billion. In China alone FinTech firms number 940 and, of these, firms working in lending have attracted 7.8 billion dollars of investments and InsurTech and FinTech credit companies account for 1.2 billion each. The 2019 PWC report (PWC 2019) shows that 4 of the 10 most important FinTech firms are Chinese and almost half of the top 100 were founded and work in emerging countries. In India, for example, where the sector has grown significantly where there are now 1650 firms, of which only 213 set up a maximum of five years ago and thus to be considered start-ups. Europe is behind as compared to the US and Asian markets but is showing significant growth rates, including in attracting funding from venture capitalists. The data from the first three months of 2019 show that Europe has achieved 15% of world venture capital funding relating to FinTech (PWC 2019).

36. Looking to the European context, an example is Funding Circle which was listed on the London Stock Exchange in late September 2018. This P2P lending platform set up in 2010 is subject to English Financial Conduct Authority supervision and works in various areas (credit broking, debt administration, debt-collecting and operating an electronic system in relation to lending) enabling investors (comprising banks, asset managers, insurers, government-backed entities and funds) to fund medium-small firms in Great Britain, the USA, Germany and the Netherlands. Since inception in 2010, in total the platform has issued 7.8 billion pounds of loans to around 60,000 small businesses, thanks to over 85,000 retail and institutional investors'. Even in markets in which FinTech development has been more limited, such as Italy, a listing process has begun. An example is Crowdfundme, an equity crowdfunding platform which launched a roadshow for its Initial Public Offering (IPO) at Alternative Investment Market (AIM) in November 2018, a process which concluded on 25 March 2019, making it the first listed Italian FinTech firm.

37. Recent cases include the merger between Finnest, an Austrian peer-to-peer lending company, and Invesdor, a Finland-based crowdfunding operator which has generated a platform which operates at the supranational level, drawing on a wider investor pool located in a range of countries (Austria, Germany, Switzerland and Northern Europe as a whole) (Reuters 2019).

38. European statistics show that lending transactions to firms and individuals account for a market value of 7.78 billion euros for a total of 1 billion transactions (www.statista.com). The growth forecast is for an average increase of 4.7% annually until 2023. Of the total, around 5.2 billion is accounted for by business contracts. The average loan to firms *via* the platforms is around 75,000 euros approximately while those to individuals average 2000 euros approximately. If we take the Italian market as an example, despite it is not having achieved full maturity, its movement's accord with these trends. In particular, with reference to FinTech activities, from 2016 to 2017 taken together such operators registered a turnover increase of 30%, reaching 118.5 million euros (PWC 2019). This sum is principally accounted for by subjects working in the payment sector (56%). Lending and crowdfunding have an overall turnover of around 19 million euros (16% of the total). Furthermore, certain statistics referring to lending crowdfunding show an average sum invested per investor of 3800 euros in the 2014–2018 period, with a maximum value of approximately 9800 euros (registered in 2014) and a minimum value of 3600 euros (in the first semester of 2018). The investor pool is also growing from 134 in 2014 to around 8300 in 2018. In reference to equity crowdfunding a significant increase in the number of issuer firms and the overall value of deals per year took place from 2016 to the first quarter of 2018 with an average sum down from 5800 to 3200 euros, reflecting a significant increase in retail investors (www.crowdfundingbuzz.it).

39. In just over two years the Borsa del Credito platform has enabled over 32 million euros to be lent to 450 SMEs, thanks to private and institutional investors.

40. ART SGR S.p.a. is authorised to manage alternative investment funds exclusively for professional investors. These funds lend money via the BorsadelCredito.it platform. Launched in October 2017 to invest in platform credit with a target of 100 million euros, Fondo Colombo was undersigned to the tune of 10 million euros by Borsa del Credito's own shareholders.

41. Workinvoice is a pure marketplace working in Italy which generated 143 million euros of business invoice funding from 2015 to 2018 on the strength of private and institutional investors. This latter included Factor@Work which buys loans on partner web platforms, securitises them and sells the securities deriving from this to professional investors.

42. Credit securitisation operations implemented by FinTech firms, already widespread abroad, are becoming more common in Italy, too. A recent example of this is the consumer credit securitisation operation implemented on the strength of a partnership between a P2P platform (Prestiamoci) and small bank (Banca Valsabbina). See Allegreni (2018).

43. As Moneyfarm reported, Vaamo's goal was further enlargement of its individual client services and digital solution provision to important European financial institutions on the strength of Vaamo's experience in its partnership with N26 and 1822direkt (online subsidiary of one of Germany's principal investment banks). The important development of the Moneyfarm platform (regulated in Italy by Consob, in the UK by the Financial Conduct Authority and in Germany by BaFin) has attracted the interest of many institutional investors: the firm's main partners are Allianz, the Cabot Square Capital investment fund, United Ventures, Endeavor and Fondazione di Sardegna.

REFERENCES

Allegreni, F. (2018, October 31). *Peer to peer lending: Prestiamoci dà il via alla prima cartolarizzazione di crediti personali [Peer to peer lending: Prestiamoci starts the first securitization of personal loans].* Retrieved March 27, 2019, from www.crowdfundingbuzz.it.

Arner, D. W., Barberis, J., & Buckley, R. P. (2016). The evolution of FinTech: New post-crisis paradigm. *Georgetown Journal of International Law, 47*(4), 1271–1320.

ASIC (Australian Securities and Investment Commission). (2017). *Survey of marketplace lending providers.* Report 256.

BaFin (Bundesanstalt für Finanzdienstleistungsaufsicht). (2018, July). *Big data meets artificial intelligence. Challenges and implications for the supervision and regulation of financial services.*

Baker, H. K., Filbeck, G., & Ricciardi, V. (Eds.). (2017). *Financial behavior: Players, services, products, and markets.* New York, NY: Oxford University Press.

Banca d'Italia. (2017, December). *FinTech in Italy. Fact-finding inquiry on the impact of financial technology on the financial, banking and insurance sectors.* Retrieved March 27, 2019, from (https://www.bancaditalia.it/compiti/vigilanza/analisi-sistema/stat-banche-intermediari/Fintech_in_Italia_2017.pdf.

Barba Navaretti, G., Calzolari, G., & Pozzolo, A. F. (2017). FinTech and banks: Friends or foes? *European Economy, 2*, 9–31.

Barbagallo, C. (2018, November 12). *Il sistema bancario italiano: situazione e prospettive [Italy's banking system: The current situation and the outlook].* Speech by the Director General for Financial Supervision and Regulation at the ASSBB, Varignana (Bologna–Italy).

BIS-FSB. (2017, May 22). *FinTech credit. Market structure, business models and financial stability implications.* Report prepared by a Working Group established by the Committee on the Global Financial System (CGFS—Bank of International Settlement) and the Financial Stability Board.

Bofondi, M. (2017). *Lending-based crowdfunding: Opportunities and risks*. Banca d'Italia Occasional Papers—Questioni di Economia e Finanza, n. 375/2017.

Capgemini-EFMA. (2017). *World FinTech report 2017*. Retrieved March 27, 2019, from www.worldfintechreport2017.com.

CB Insights. (2017). *Big Tech in AI: What Amazon, Apple, Google, GE, and others are working on*.

CGFS and FSB. (2017, May 22). *FinTech credit: Market structure, business models and financial stability implications*. Committee on the Global Financial System (CGFS) and Financial Stability Board (FSB).

Claessens, S., Frost, J., Turner, G., & Zhu, F. (2018, September). Fintech credit markets around the world: Size, drivers and policy issues. *BIS Quarterly Review*.

Consob–OCF–Università Roma Tre–GFK. (2017). *La relazione consulente-cliente, Addendum al Rapporto Consob sulle scelte finanziarie delle famiglie italiane [The consultant-client relationship, Addendum to the Consob Report on the financial choices of Italian families]*.

Di Mascio, A. (2018). *Wealth management e Fintech. Le nuove sfide tra Private Banker e Robo Advisor [Wealth Management and Fintech. The new challenges between Private Banker and Robo Advisor]*. Milan: Egea.

EBA. (2017, August 4). *Discussion paper on the EBA's approach to financial technology (FinTech)*. EBA/DP/2017/02.

EBA. (2018, July 3). *EBA report on the impact of Fintech on incumbent credit institutions' business models*.

ECB. (2018, June). *Survey on the access to finance of enterprises in the euro area*.

EIOPA. (2017). *EIOPA InsurTech Roundtable. How technology and data are reshaping the insurance landscape*.

ESAs. (2018, September 5). *Joint Committee report on the results of the monitoring exercise on 'automation in financial advice'*. JC 2018/29.

European Commission. (2018, March 8). *Proposal for a regulation of the European Parliament and of the council on European Crowdfunding Service Providers (ECSP) for business*. COM(2018) 113 final, 2018/0048 (COD), Brussels.

Federal Reserve Banks. (2017). *Small business credit survey*. Report on employer firms.

Financial Times. (2018, October 22). *UK peer-to-peer lender asks regulator for help*.

Finextra. (2019, March 26). *Satispay passports out of London with Luxembourg licence*. Retrieved April 1, 2019, from https://www.finextra.com/pressarticle/77790/satispay-passports-out-of-london-with-luexembourg-licence/retail.

Forbes. (2019, February 5). *A major bitcoin exchange has a serious problem*. Retrieved from bit.ly/2TwL4x1.

FSB. (2017a, June 27). *Financial stability implications from FinTech, supervisory and regulatory issues that merit authorities' attention*.

FSB. (2017b, May 10). *Global shadow banking monitoring report 2016.* Financial Stability Board.

FSB. (2018, March 5). *Global shadow banking monitoring report 2017.* Financial Stability Board.

Fujitsu. (2018). Digitalization is not a "threat" but an "opportunity"——The future of financial services delivered by FinTech. *Fujitsu Journal.* Retrieved from https://journal.jp.fujitsu.com/en/2018/07/11/01/.

Gobbi, G. (2016). *The troubled life of the banking industry, European Association of University Teachers of Banking and Finance.* Wolpertinger conference 2016, Verona. Retrieved March 27, 2019, from https://www.bancaditalia.it/pubblicazioni/interventi-vari/int-var-2016/Gobbi_02092016.pdf.

Hau, H., Huang, Y., Shan, H., & Sheng, Z. (2017). *TechFin in China: Credit market completion and its growth effect.* BFER 6th annual conference, Singapore.

Jakšič, M., & Marinc, M. (2015). The future of banking: The role of information technology. *Bančni Vestnik, 64*(11), 68–73.

Kirby, E., & Worner, S. (2014). *Crowd-funding: An infant industry growing fast.* Staff working paper of the IOSCO Research Department, SWP3/2014.

Liberti, J. M., & Petersen, M. A. (2018, August). *Information: Hard and soft.* WP. https://www.kellogg.northwestern.edu/faculty/petersen/htm/papers/hard%20and%20soft%20information.pdf.

Nakaso, H. (2017, November 1). *Big data—Its impacts on economies, finance and central banking.* Remarks at the Fourth FinTech Forum of Deputy Governor of the Bank of Japan.

OECD. (2018). *Financial markets, insurance and pensions, digitalisation and finance.* Retrieved March 27, 2019, from http://www.oecd.org/finance/privatepensions/Financial-markets-insurance-pensions-digitalisation-and-finance.pdf.

OICV-IOSCO. (2017, February). *IOSCO research report on financial technologies (Fintech).*

Pia, P. (2017). *La consulenza finanziaria automatizzata* [Automated financial advice], Franco Angeli, Milano.

PWC. (2017). *The state of FinTech.* Retrieved from https://www.pwc.com/sg/en/publications/assets/fintech-startupbootcamp-state-of-fintech-2017.pdf.

PWC. (2018). *Le aziende del Fintech in Italia nel 2017* [Fintech companies in Italy in 2017]. Retrieved March 27, 2019, from https://www.pwc.com/it/it/industries/fintech/docs/2017-fintech-report.pdf.

PWC. (2019). *Piccole FinTech crescono con "intelligenza"* [Small FinTechs grow with "intelligence"]. Retrieved March 28, 2019, from https://www.pwc.com/it/it/publications/assets/docs/PwC-FinTech.pdf.

Reuters. (2019, March 19). *Finnish crowdfunding firm invesdor buys Austrian peer, seeks M&A.* Retrieve April 1, 2019, from https://www.reuters.com/article/us-invesdor-growth/finnish-crowdfunding-firm-invesdor-buys-austrian-peer-seeks-ma-idUSKCN1R02SC.

Rooney, K. (2018, November 16). PayPal and Square quietly grow small business lending using data as their edge over banks. *CNBC*. Retrieved March 28, 2019, from https://www.cnbc.com.

Schena, C., Tanda, A., Arlotta, C., & Potenza, G. (2018, March). *The development of FinTech. Opportunities and risks for the financial industry in the digital era*. Consob—FinTech papers, no. 1. Retrieved March 28, 2019, from http://www.consob.it/web/area-pubblica/ftl.

Scopsi, M. (2018). *The expansion of big data companies in the financial services industry, and EU regulation*. IAI papers 19/06.

Sperimborgo, S. (2016). *Banche e innovazione tecnologica. Come avere successo nella tempesta perfetta della rivoluzione digitale [Banks and technological innovation. How to succeed in the perfect storm of the digital revolution]*. Bancaria, n. 12.

Viacom. (2013). *The millennial disruption index*. Retrieved March 28, 2019, from https://www.bbva.com/wp-content/uploads/2015/08/millenials.pdf.

World Bank Group and the People's Bank of China. (2018). *Toward universal financial inclusion in China: Models, challenges, and global lessons*. Retrieved March 28, 2019, from https://responsiblefinanceforum.org/wp-content/uploads/2018/04/FinancialInclusionChinaP158554.pdf.

Worthington, S., & Welch, P. (2010). Banking without the banks. *International Journal of Bank Marketing, 29*(2), 190–201. Retrieved March 28, 2019, from https://doi.org/10.1108/02652321111107657.

Zetzsche, D. A., Buckley, R. P., Arner, D. W., & Barberis, J. N. (2017). *From FinTech to TechFin: The regulatory challenges of data-driven finance*. EBI working paper series, no. 6.

CHAPTER 3

BigTech Strategic Approaches: Worrying Competition?

Abstract By leveraging on the data acquired within their core businesses, BigTech firms have long offered financial services too, starting with payment services and continuing with lending and wealth management services. Strategies involving widening financial services provision can be implemented according to two main development lines: development to support the main core business or development to diversify the services offered. US and Chinese BigTechs, in particular, are offering an ever increasing number and wider set of products on the market, including via the creation of controlled dedicated financial intermediaries, to allow them to respond to customers' needs with a holistic approach.

Keywords BigTech • Big data • Financial conglomerate • Financial services

3.1   BigTech's Competitive Potential

The analysis carried out in the previous chapters highlighted that the competitive threat exerted by FinTech as regards the traditional financial system is credible and pervasive and this is even more true of TechFin companies. As the TechFin companies have grown in size and popularity, in fact, they have enjoyed a large database and the consolidated trust of their clients (FSB 2019).

© The Author(s) 2019   37
A. Tanda, C.-M. Schena, *FinTech, BigTech and Banks*, Palgrave
Macmillan Studies in Banking and Financial Institutions,
https://doi.org/10.1007/978-3-030-22426-4_3

To this should be added that the TechFin firms, and above all BigTech companies, possess the huge financial resources required to expand their activities.[1] The BigTech firms can thus formulate financial sector entry strategies without having to take particular balance-sheet constraints into account and also have the investment potential for much more significant technological improvements than most of the banks and financial intermediaries. Moreover, the BigTech firms have, for some time, possessed more advanced technology[2] and continue to invest in technological innovation research. Incumbent firms are thus hindered by scalability problems linked to the entity of technological investments and the ability to attract talent, key factors for development and efficiency increases in financial services too, and to measure up competitively with the BigTech firms. Moreover, the effect of competition with BigTech firms may be to reduce traditional operators' profit margins as well as their ability to cross-subsidise products (FSB 2019).

Whilst only some of the BigTech firms are international in scope, with the others operating mainly in domestic markets (USA, United Kingdom, European Union or EU, China, etc.) or neighbouring countries, it is plausible to hypothesise that, over time, these latter may expand their sphere of action further, not only with the aim of increasing client numbers but also in order to "follow" their long-term clients in their financial needs where these expand abroad. This scenario seems likely because, as we have seen, a key element in digital strategy is customer experience, understood as clients' overall experience in their dealings with the firm in question. BigTech firms are thus interested not only in the "shopping" experience on their client platforms but, first and foremost, in a relationship based on customer care and support as well as interaction with the brand. In other words, clients must have all their needs satisfied by a single interlocutor who knows how to simplify access to services and even forecast client needs and anticipate their responses. Part of BigTech's success is, in fact, due to new client demands—which incumbent firms are incapable of responding to—and the ability of the new generation to access technological services (Carstens 2018). Note, also, that whilst FinTech users are largely retail, BigTech's core business means that its customers encompasses a multiplicity of firms which they work with or which offer goods and services on their platforms.

It is, thus, in this context that BigTech's choices are to be interpreted as such firms were set up in their respective operational areas (e-commerce, computer and telephones, search engines, social media, internet services and digital games) which they have, over time, decided to diversify out of, including into financial services. The next section will examine this issue.

3.2 BigTech Financial Services Development Strategies

An in-depth study of BigTech's choices on how to enter the financial sector and develop their activities can act as the basis for a consideration of BigTech's financial services development strategies. Table 3.1 shows six of the principal market players most active in the financial sector for whom comparable public information is available, namely US Google, Apple, Facebook and Amazon (GAFA) and Chinese Tencent and Alibaba.

A first indication which can be drawn from Table 3.1 is the diverse financial activity spheres (payment, lending and wealth management services) in which BigTech works, with payment services being the prevalent sector, at least in volume terms. Credit is also an especially important area for BigTech and TechFin firms. With exclusive reference to FinTech credit, the Bank for International Settlements has highlighted that, in some countries such as Brazil and Argentina, TechFin firms have achieved highly significant credit volumes, exceeding those of FinTech (Carstens 2018; Frost et al. 2019).

Table 3.1 also shows that individual services can be offered in different geographical areas and in a number of countries which do not necessarily coincide with those in which BigTech firms carry out their original activities. Moreover, this aspect may reflect a precise operational choice (prompted by the desire to penetrate only certain markets with financial services) as much as a not yet complete strategy designed to gradually extend financial services to all the geographical areas in which BigTech works. In this latter case, then, a further expansion of services can be expected, which may progressively expand into markets in which BigTech's clients work, in accordance with the previously cited "follow clients" logic. A further consideration is also worthy of note—as it is certainly capable of impacting on geographical positioning choices—that, in the various countries in which BigTech develops its core business, there may be more or less clear and/or incisive or onerous regulatory provisions on financial activities.

On the strategic level, moreover, it is clear that financial services provision is, in most cases, the result of in-house development. The services and products conceived by BigTech firms are offered and distributed via subsidiaries and associates (shown with an S in Table 3.1). Where required in the various operational reference markets these group firms are authorised to operate as regulated financial intermediaries. Moreover, in many cases financial services provision also takes place on the basis of partnership agreements.

Table 3.1 BigTech's financial sector development strategies

Financial activities	Name	Year of founding	Parent company registered offices	Core business	Primary financial sector development strategy	Principal financial services offered (directly, by the group's firms or in partnerships)	The group's financial intermediaries (S) or partners and supervisory authorities with geographical jurisdiction	Geographical working sphere
Payment services in support of core business	Apple	1977	USA	IT and telephones	In-house development Services offered via: • subsidiary or controlled companies; • partnerships	Payment (Apple Pay) and money transfer services: Apple Pay cash Apple Card (planned)	Makes use of partner payment circuit and banking partnerships around the world Apple Payments (S) is an authorised money transmitter in the USA	The USA and a further 28 countries
	Facebook	2004	USA	Social network	In-house development Services offered via: • subsidiary or controlled companies; • partnerships	Payment and money transfer services: Facebook payments	In the USA, authorised money transmitters in the various states Facebook Payments International Limited is regulated as an electronic currency institution by the Central Bank of Ireland	USA Europe
	Google	1998	USA	Search engine and internet services	In-house development Services offered via: • subsidiary or controlled companies; • partnerships	Payment and money transfer services: Google pay	In the USA, authorised money transmitters in the various states In Europe, it works together with the Nexi circuit linked with personal credit cards. The subsidiary Google Payments is an authorised e-money provider in Europe	Payments: 70 countries for online purchases and 20 for physical shop purchases Money transfers: USA and UK Public transport ticket purchase: 6 countries

Payment and lending services in support of core business	Amazon	1994	USA	e-commerce	In-house development Services offered via: • subsidiary or controlled companies • partnerships	Payment services: Amazon Pay and Amazon Cash Lending services: Amazon Credit—including with revolving solutions	Amazon Pay is an authorised Money Transmitter in the USA. The subsidiary Amazon Payments Europe is an authorised payment institution in Luxembourg and supervised by Commission de Surveillance du Secteur Financier (CSSF) Amazon Credit services are offered in partnership with a bank (Synchrony Bank)	Over 170 countries Amazon Cash only available in the USA USA, Japan and UK
Financial services to diversify business	Tencent	1998	China	Internet services, games and software	Development of financial services by specially created subsidiaries	Payment services: Tenpay Weixin/WeChat Pay, QQ Wallet Banking services: WeBank	WeBank: authorised as a bank in China	China (and Chinese clients abroad)
	Alibaba	1999	China	e-commerce	Development of financial services by specially created subsidiaries	Payment services, lending to small businesses, consumer credit, own and partner investment funds: Ant Financial Banking services: MYbank	Ant Financial is an authorised bank in China (previously known as Alipay) MYbank (controlled by Ant Financial) is an authorised bank in China	China (and Chinese clients abroad)

Source: Our elaboration of information drawn from the websites of the parent company and its subsidiaries (updated in March 2019)

Overall, our analysis brings out the two different strategic approaches currently used for financial sector development with the first of these essentially targeting provisions of financial services instrumental to reinforcing a firm's core business and the second having a more market activity diversification objective, implemented via the creation of complex and variously structured conglomerates.

3.2.1   Core Business Reinforcement Strategies

This strategic approach is that which US GAFA have adopted to date. On the basis of the contents of Table 3.1 we can highlight the following.

In order to operate on the domestic market, Apple, Facebook and Google have developed in-house payment tools, activating money transmitter or payment institution licences. Apple recently (March 2019) announced its intention of activating a credit card service in partnership with Goldman Sachs. Apple Card is a virtual credit card to be used from the Apple Pay app and integrated into Apple Wallet, whose launch is planned for this summer although the details and economic conditions have not yet been released (Financial Times 2019).

Facebook applied for a licence to work in Europe via a subsidiary company authorised as an electronic money institution in Ireland as far back as 2016. Google has also recently applied for a licence for its subsidiary Google Payments from the Lithuanian authorities (Seputyte and Kahn 2018) to set up its own services in Europe. Furthermore, on their foreign markets, Apple and Google offer payment services in partnership with banks, consumer credit institutions and existing payment circuits.

Amazon first developed payment systems to favour rapid and simple purchase payments on its website and subsequently began offering lending services for both consumers (via traditional or revolving credit cards) and the small businesses which sell their products via the Amazon website. These latter can access an international shop window with positive effects for sales volumes via e-commerce. In 2016, there were around 33 million Amazon Pay clients in 170 nations. Amazon's lending service—now active in the USA, Japan and the UK—has supplied 3 billion dollars in loans and benefits from a partnership between the e-commerce platform and Bank of America Merrill Lynch.[3]

On the basis of this approach, in the cases referred to above, it can be noted that financial services provision is strictly functional to the strengthening of BigTech's core business. In fact, for a company active in e-commerce

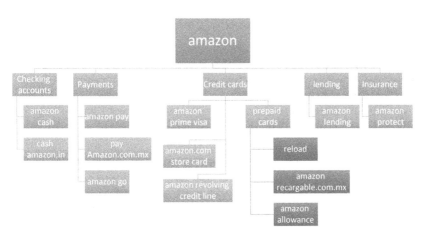

Fig. 3.1 Financial products and services offered through Amazon. Source: Authors' elaboration on CB Insights (2018a)

in goods and services, being able to offer payment tools and small loans supporting clients in making purchases enables sales volumes to be increased and can determine an increase in client numbers and types. Note that the unbundling of financial services enables this strategic approach to be developed without recourse to banking licences and frequently without subjecting the firm to supervision on its financial activities, depending on the legal framework of the countries it works in.

At the same time, clients see the BigTech firm as capable of satisfying their needs including the financial ones. In this sense, the map of the financial, insurance and pension services offered by Amazon (Fig. 3.1) is illustrative, echoing the structure of a complex banking group whilst this is not the legal solution adopted by the BigTech. Amazon, in fact, uses partnerships rather than acquiring firms for the development of its financial services in its main reference markets (USA and India). As has been effectively underlined: "It's hard to claim that Amazon is building the next-generation bank. But it's clear that the company remains very focused on building financial services products that support its core strategic goal: increasing participation in the Amazon ecosystem. In a sense, Amazon is building a bank for itself—and that may be an even more compelling development than the company launching a deposit-holding bank. Amazon had discussions about offering insurance in conjunction with its connected home devices" (CB Insights 2018).

3.2.2   Business Diversification Strategies

In other cases, BigTech firms have considered it opportune to pursue intense diversification strategies, even going as far as to set up a bank and a finance group within their industrial group. This is the case of Chinese Tencent and Alibaba, now leading financial conglomerates which develop especially significant financial activity volumes. Table 3.1 can be used as the basis on which to highlight the main strategic choices made by these two BigTech firms.

Tencent is a Chinese holding company working mainly in entertainment services, mass media, internet and communications. In addition to payment applications developed many years ago, Tencent set up WeBank in 2015, one of China's first authorised online banks (Financial Times 2015).[4] The WeBank brand name echoes the name of Tencent's famous messaging app WeChat. The bank principally offers the products of other financial intermediaries and grants its own small size consumer loans on its Weilidai platform (Citigroup 2018). The bank has many partnerships with a range of Chinese financial intermediaries including banks, insurance companies and asset management firms and these agreements enable WeBank to distribute its partner banks' products to its own clients.

In the FinTech context, Tencent makes its profits from various sources including payment services, wallets and consumer credit (Table 3.2). Tencent also manages an asset management platform called LiCaiTong whose asset under management value was estimated in January 2018, to be 300 billion yuan (47.4 billion dollars) (Xiao 2018). In October 2017, Tencent obtained a licence to distribute insurance products and began activating partnerships in this context (Tencent 2018).

Moving on to Alibaba, this BigTech launched its own financial sector entry strategy in 2004, on the basis of Alipay, a FinTech firm specialising in payments.[5] Alipay's services were initially supplied on the basis of partnerships with certain Chinese banks. In 2011, it obtained a payment services licence from the People's Bank of China and in 2012, a third-party payment platform for fund transactions from China Securities Regulatory Commission. In 2013, Alipay entered a partnership with Chinese Tianhong Asset Management enabling its clients to invest in the Yu'e Bao investment fund which enables small scale savers to earn from their savings. The fund originated as an Alipay client support service on which clients can set aside residual sums from payments made using its app. In

Table 3.2 Main FinTech services offered by Tencent

Service	Description	Year of activation or foundation	Monetisation	User base
Tenpay	Payment solution—it is the second largest online payment platform in China	2005	N.a.	N.a.
Weixin Pay	Payment solution enabling quick payment transactions on mobile phones, based on Swift payments connected to bank cards	2013	Free; withdrawal fees (RMB1/1000); Commission fees (0.6%–2%)	Over 800 million Mobile Payments (including both Weixin Pay and QQ Wallet) monthly active user accounts (2Q18)
QQ Wallet	Mobile payment product incorporating multiple payment methods such as bank card payments, QR code payments and NFC payments	N.a.	Free; Commission fees (0.6%–2%)	
LiCaiTong	Wealth management platform, accessible via the WeChat wallet	2014	Commission	Not disclosed
Weilidai (affiliate WeBank)	Unsecured consumer loan business	2015	Interest rate (annualised 18%)	Not disclosed
WeSure (subsidiary)	Proprietary insurance platform	2017	Free; commission	Not disclosed

Note: 2Q18 stands for second quarter 2018

Source: Re-elaboration from Tencent, Investor Kit, Product List (without data) http://www.tencent.com/en-us/investor.html#info_performance; https://www.tencent.com/en-us/system.html and Tencent (2018)

this way, clients could access money funds in a very simple way, using their smartphones. Its success was a watershed moment (UBS 2018): in September 2018, the Yu'e Bao fund's asset under management value amounted to 200 billion dollars making it the largest monetary fund in the world.[6] The return offered is higher than those from a yearly deposit (Carstens 2018).

In 2014, Alibaba set up Ant Financial Services Group, which originated from Alipay. Ant Financial obtained a banking licence in China and leads the Alibaba group's financial sub-holding company. In the context of this sub-holding company, Ant Financial set up MYbank in 2014, which obtained a banking licence and operates exclusively online. Ant Financial offers lending, cash management and insurance services in the domestic market as well as payment services for Chinese clients the world over. The bank equipped itself with especially efficient tools and procedures to respond rapidly and effectively to client demands. For example, getting credit requires clients to fill in a three-minute application form which provides a response in a second (positively or negatively) (Ant Financial 2018a). The data presented to investors in 2018, showed that, in a single year, the number of users making use of at least two of the firm's financial services had grown from 430 million in 2017 to 640 million in August 2018. Its lending, cash management and insurance policy services are used, respectively, by 11, 21 and 40 million small businesses.

In May 2018, Ant Financial included a further two funds managed by asset management partners in its services (Bosera Asset Management Co., Ltd., and Zhong Ou Asset Management Co., Ltd.) with all Alibaba group clients being able to invest in these (Ant Financial 2018b). In the context of the financial system, then, the Alibaba group competes with incumbent firms but has also, in various cases, managed to attract certain important financial partners. It is also now technological services provider to incumbent firms. In 2018, Ant Financial launched a tech company, Ant Financial Technology, focusing on the development of technological solutions for financial services which are offered to the clients of the whole Alibaba group. In its first months of business Ant Financial Technology's products were already extremely successful and had been bought up by over 100 banks, 60 insurance companies and over 40 wealth management and broker firms (Ant Financial 2018c).

3.3   DEVELOPMENT AND COMPETITIVE COMPARISON PROSPECTS

Overall this analysis highlights an intense development in financial activities and the generally innovative services provision methods enacted by BigTech firms which tend to interpret financial services as "commodities" which can be offered clients via exclusively digital and automated solutions. At the same time, the primary objective which emerges from their strategic choices is the creation of integrated service platforms which enable BigTech to become a single reference point for clients' various needs.[7] This goal seems a credible one, not solely in consideration of the significant technological and financial resources which BigTech firms possess but also their ability to respond to an ever wider range of financial demands from a growing number of clients. This enables BigTech firms to operate on the market on a par with the largest incumbent firms right from the start.

We have also highlighted that, whilst setting up a bank requires obtaining a licence from supervisory bodies,[8] when the latter is not considered opportune or worthwhile it is, in any case, possible to work in the banking sector offering clients a multiplicity of financial services in competition with regulated financial intermediaries. A comparison between Alibaba and Amazon is illustrative of this.

It can also be observed that the diversification and innovation offered by BigTech (and also FinTech) digital platforms is implemented via unbundling and rebundling mechanisms. It is, in fact, thanks to unbundling that the financial services offered to clients no longer falls within the traditional, rigid perimeters of financial services demarcation (banking, financial and insurance) but via processes and markets which are frequently not subject to supervisory norms on a par with those applying to financial intermediaries. Platforms thus emerge from a single financial function but, via the rebundling of the services offered by a multiplicity of financial firms and operators, succeed in selecting and combining only the services required by their clients and offering these as "new" financial products.[9]

To date, whatever the strategic approach adopted, all BigTechs have sought out partnerships with some of the principal international incumbent firms (banks, investment funds, etc.) in order to progressively reinforce and expand their financial activities. However, competition within the financial system may increase further also in consideration of the considerable digital replicability of the majority of financial services, especially on the basis of an unbundling process which breaks up traditional financial intermediation's value chain and enables new digital operators to exploit the most profitable or least burdensome phases of the process in terms of risk exposure and legal compliance.

Furthermore, competition can be more intense the higher the product and service standardisation (not solely lending but also investment), targeting retail clients (individuals and small and medium-sized enterprises) in consideration of the greater replicability and thus interchangeability, of the products and services offered by the various types of financial operators (banks, BigTech and FinTech).

NOTES

1. An insight into the size of this financial capacity is provided, for example, by the fact that if Ant Financial (the bank set up within the Alibaba group) were to be listed on the stock exchange it would be one of the top ten banks internationally in terms of market capitalisation and that the Alibaba group's capitalisation is superior to that of the principal international banking groups (JP Morgan Chase, ICBC, Bank of America, Wells Fargo, etc.) (Carstens 2018).

2. A clear example is artificial intelligence (AI), in which the main BigTech firms are world leaders.

3. Press releases indicate that the partnership with Merrill Lynch could be extended to fund businesses which are not part of its marketplaces. Amazon has also made contact with JP Morgan to assess the potential for offering its clients current accounts (Financial Times 2018).

4. As the WeBank site shows, the bank has been authorised since December 2014, under the name Shenzhen Qianhai Weizhong Bank Co., Ltd.

5. See https://www.antfin.com/history.htm.

6. The size of this investment fund, offered by Ant Financial, and the funds offered by Tencent's subsidiaries has worried the Chinese regulatory authorities which saw some of the marketing techniques used by the funds as unethical as regards investors. These latter effectively prompted investors to perceive these solutions as alternative but equivalent tools to liquid deposits without investors being properly informed of the risks linked to investing in these funds. According to the Chinese market regulation authority, the China Securities Regulatory Commission, this mistaken perception of the risks by investors could potentially cause a liquidity crisis with consequences for the stability of the whole Chinese financial system at such time as savers may decide to shift their money from bank deposits to these monetary funds. The authority thus considered it useful to set out an annual redemption limit for monetary funds in order to limit cash flows from bank accounts and make the difference between the two financial tools in terms of liquidity availability more evident (Carstens 2018; Reuters 2018; UBS 2018).

7. The German Federal control authorities have published a study on the implications for financial services of the interaction between big data (BD) and artificial intelligence systems highlighting that the combination of these information elaboration systems (BDAI) constitutes a powerfully innovative factor for the financial system and may generate monopolistic formations by the large technological operators. Furthermore, standardisation of the lion's share of financial activities might potentially lead to further expansion of dependency on information providers (BaFin 2018).

8. In this respect note that, in 2018, the European Central Bank updated its guidelines for the issuing of permits to provide banking services (ECB 2018a) and drew up a separate document focusing on FinTech lending bodies (ECB 2018b). Whilst, in its note accompanying the guidelines, the ECB specified that the FinTech banks are subject to the same regulations expected of other "traditional" banks, the contents of the guidelines specify additional requisites for FinTech lending bodies. We would argue that this may discourage FinTech firms from applying for banking licences in the European context and prompt them to continue to do business using the solutions used to date. For further consideration of this, see Sect. 5.2.

9. Rebundling is a method involving unbundling financial products provided by various companies, and selecting and combining only the services consumers need, offering them as new financial products (Fujitsu Journal 2018). The rebundling process translates into a customer-centric experience involving a high degree of collaboration (WSBI-ESBG 2018).

References

Ant Financial. (2018a, September 17–18). *2018 investor day. Ant financial—The global leading FinTech company.*

Ant Financial. (2018b, May 3). *Alipay introduces two new money market funds to Yu'e Bao platform.* Retrieved March 27, 2019, from https://www.antfin.com/newsDetail.html?id=5b0d697b623e7f7c82e661e8.

Ant Financial. (2018c, September 20). *Ant Financial launches Ant Financial Technology brand with full suite of technology products and services to support growth of financial institutions.* Retrieved March 27, 2019, from https://www.antfin.com/newsDetail.html?id=5ba34944f07d7acfc335da0d.

BaFin (Bundesanstalt für Finanzdienstleistungsaufsicht). (2018, July). *Big data meets artificial intelligence. Challenges and implications for the supervision and regulation of financial services.*

Carstens, A. (2018, December 4). *Big tech in finance and new challenges for public policy.* Keynote address by the General Manager, Bank for International Settlements, FT Banking Summit, London.

CB Insights. (2018). *Everything you need to know about what Amazon is doing in financial services.*

Citigroup. (2018, March). *Bank of the future. The ABCs of digital disruption in finance.* Citi GPS: Global Perspectives and Solutions.

ECB. (2018a, March). *Guide to assessments of licence applications. Licence applications in general.*

ECB. (2018b, March). *Guide to assessments of fintech credit institution licence applications.*

Financial Times. (2015, gennaio 5). *Tencent launches China's first online-only bank.*

Financial Times. (2018, March 5). *Amazon in talks with JPMorgan to offer bank accounts.*

Financial Times. (2019, March 26). *Goldman's Apple Card launch leaves questions unanswered.* Retrieved March 27, 2019, from https://www.ft.com/content/2d7051f8-4f51-11e9-b401-8d9ef1626294.

Frost, J., Gambacorta, L., Huang, Y., Shin, H. S., & Zbinden, P. (2019). *Big Tech and the changing structure of financial intermediation.* BIS working paper, 779, April 2019.

FSB. (2019, February 14). *FinTech and market structure in financial services: Market developments and potential financial stability implications.*

Fujitsu Journal. (2018). Digitalization is not a "threat" but an "opportunity"—The future of financial services delivered by FinTech. *Fujitsu Journal.* https://journal.jp.fujitsu.com/en/2018/07/11/01/.

Reuters. (2018, giugno 1). *China steps up regulation of fast-growing money market funds.* Retrieved March 27, 2019, from https://www.reuters.com/article/us-china-funds-moneymarket/china-steps-up-regulation-of-fast-growing-money-market-funds-idUSKCN1IX4FZ.

Seputyte, M., & Kahn, J. (2018). *Google payment expands with e-money license from Lithuania.* Retrieved March 28, 2019, from https://www.bloomberg.com/news/articles/2018-12-21/google-payment-expands-with-e-money-license-from-lithuania.

Tencent. (2018). *Annual report 2017.* http://www.tencent.com/en-us/articles/17000391523362601.pdf.

UBS. (2018, May 29). *China's money market reforms.* Retrieved March 27, 2019, from https://www.ubs.com/microsites/china-insights/en/insights/fixed-income/2018/china-money-market-reform.html.

WSBI-ESBG. (2018). Proportionality helps banks, banking workforce. *News and Views,* Q3. https://www.wsbi-esbg.org/SiteCollectionDocuments/9492_PER_NEWSVIEWS_2_2018.pdf.

Xiao, L. (2018). *Tencent money-market fund triples in three years.* Retrieved March 27, 2019, from https://www.caixinglobal.com/2018-03-22/tencent-money-market-fund-triples-in-three-years-101224888.html.

CHAPTER 4

Bank Strategies in the Light of the Digitalisation of Financial Activities

Abstract Incumbent firms are responding to the challenges of digitalisation by adopting a number of strategies. The large international banks are implementing a mixed strategy that includes shareholdings in FinTech companies, partnerships and also in-house development in the different areas of financial intermediation that are being affected by technological innovation. Many initiatives focus on lending, online banking and payments but wealth management and support technologies for middle and back office are also in place. The degree of disruption caused by the initiatives varies, with many banks mainly focusing on the digitalisation of channels. Smaller banks face additional constraints because of their limited size and investment potential, together with their traditional link with the territory they operate in and their traditional approach to customers. Digitalisation has become a key issue for these intermediaries, too, if they are to be able to cope with competition not only from FinTechs and BigTechs but also from larger incumbents and new entrants. Of the latter, digital native banks have started to operate successfully on the market through innovative business models and by offering highly digitalised content and services, which meet customers' expectations. These can be created by incumbent firms, new entrants or BigTech conglomerate spin-offs.

Keywords Incumbent firms • Banks • Digital transformation • Digital disruption • Strategy

© The Author(s) 2019
A. Tanda, C.-M. Schena, *FinTech, BigTech and Banks*, Palgrave Macmillan Studies in Banking and Financial Institutions, https://doi.org/10.1007/978-3-030-22426-4_4

51

4.1   Digital Transformation and Digital Disruption

A recent analysis by the European Banking Authority (EBA 2018) has underlined two trends (digital transformation and digital disruption) in the context of the multiplicity of strategic approaches adopted by the banks in the new digitalisation context, highlighting that these involve a different level of organisational and business model change. In the case of digital transformation, banks implement a, generally in-house, strategy based on digital channel creation, which essentially targets procedure digitalisation and optimisation, thus reducing costs and improving efficiency. The ultimate goal of the digital disruption approach is instead to seek out new profit sources and fulfil new clients' demands. The EBA (2018) has also highlighted that the banks have, in some cases, themselves created native digital banks within their groups and, in other cases, are reworking the whole organisational, productive and distributional structure in a digital direction.

The public information available does not enable us to fully assess the degree of innovation involved and this is even truer of the effectiveness of the strategies adopted by the individual banks, also in consideration of the fact that many of these have only recently been implemented. We consider further study of the various approaches used to date at an international level by banks of various sizes and operational vocation to be useful nonetheless. This will enable us not only to more fully understand the positioning of the European financial system, as compared to the international framework, but also, and above all, to acquire further elements facilitating an assessment of the banking activities business model forecast scenarios.

4.2   The Strategic Choices of Large Banks: The Path Towards "Bank Tech"

This analysis of the strategies of the large banks is based on our own database made up of a sample of 32 incumbent firms, 24 of which are European, on the basis of which it has been possible to acquire significant information for the purposes of this analysis.[1] Thus defined, the sample includes a significant number of the main banks operating internationally and which have been especially active in the digitalisation process.[2] The evidence which has emerged from our analysis enables us to distinguish between initiatives designed to develop financial intermediation activities (loans, personal finance, trading platforms, wealth management, payments, insurance services, etc.), on one hand, and technological activities functional or instrumental to financial activities (blockchain systems, data analytics, security, compliance and data protection, RegTech,[3] etc.), on the other. Furthermore, the intensity of incumbent activities has been highlighted in each of these contexts and measured by the number of banks which have activated digitalisation initiatives, adopting a range of strategic approaches, namely through shareholdings, forming partnerships and in-house development.

In the first case (shareholding), this classification enables incumbent firms implementing majority and minority stakeholding strategies in FinTech and Tech firms (directly or via subsidiaries or venture capital funds) to be examined. In this category, we have included shares acquisitions in native digital banks originally made up of third-party bodies (FinTech or other). Partnerships, on the other hand, identify joint working via agreements and alliances for the development of new products or services or for the distribution of financial products and services via digital channels. In-house development relates to initiatives developed by banks themselves, or by their groups, and encompasses both business digitalisation strategies (front, middle and back office) in sales and distribution channels and the creation of subsidiaries within the group expressly focusing on digital development. These latter also include online banks set up new within a banking group.

Table 4.1 contains a synthesis of our analysis, enabling the intensity of the initiatives developed by the large banks to be understood with reference to the various digital development ambits.

The first indication which emerges from Table 4.1 is that no area of activity in which a single strategic approach is used by the sample banks exists. Considering the level of intensity of the initiatives, it is clear that the banks, in general, have paid special attention to digital developments in payment services which, as we have seen, constitute FinTech's original area of development and have been widely developed by BigTech firms. In this area, the banks have adopted various strategic approaches: 17 banks (14 of which are European) have acquired shareholdings in FinTech firms, 8 banks (7 of which are European) have entered partnerships and 11 banks (9 of which are European) have developed in-house projects. Interest by incumbent firms in blockchain type technologies is also extremely high. In this context, 23 of the sample's banks (19 of which are European) have invested in Tech companies and 1 European bank has activated a partnership with a Tech company.

Table 4.1   International bank digital development strategies

Area of development		Development strategy					
		Shareholding		Partnership		In-house	
		E	I	E	I	E	I
Financial intermediation activities	Lending and financing	6	4	3	1	7	
	Personal finance, including online banking services (*)	5	3	1		12	2
	Corporate banking services					2	
	Trading	9	4			3	1
	Wealth management	5	3	5	2	10	3
	Payments	14	3	7	1	9	2
	InsurTech	2	3			6	
Technological, functional or instrumental activities	Blockchain	19	4	1			
	Data analytics	6	4	3		2	2
	Security, compliance and data protection	2				8	2
	RegTech	7	4	1			

From low to high number of initiatives

The number of incumbent firms activating at least one initiative within the business sphere concerned is shown in each box. The total is higher than the sample total because individual banks activate a range of strategies in various spheres.

(*) The term "online banking" identifies: 1) current and savings account management services mainly for retail clients via which balances can be consulted and the main banking functions used; 2) development of exclusively online current accounts; 3) creation or development of new digital banks principally offering savings services in current accounts.

Source: The authors' own elaborations

Further considerations can be made on the basis of an examination of the various types of strategic solutions adopted.

Acquiring shareholdings in FinTech and Tech companies is the most frequently used strategy for the development of most of the financial and instrumental services. It is plausible that this is a result of a desire on the part of the banks to identify rapid and immediate operational solutions for the development of specific operational areas in which FinTech and Tech firms have now acquired great expertise and developed more advanced technological solutions. In particular, it is clear that this solution has been adopted especially frequently in payment services development (17 cases of which 14 by European banks) and blockchain (23 cases, 19 of which are European).

In-house development applies to the majority of banks in the personal finance and online banking area focusing principally on retail clients (14 cases, 12 of which are European banks), wealth management (13 cases, 10 of which are European banks) and security, compliance and data protection (10 cases, 8 of which are European). This would seem to show a desire on the part of the large banks—both European and non-European—to move on to internal development of the main core business areas and those of greatest added value as well as activities linked to the internal supervision system which is of strategic importance in client relations.

Partnerships were resorted to in a smaller number of cases and related primarily to payment services (8 cases, only one of which was a non-European bank) and wealth management (7 cases, 5 of which were European). This solution is thus considered secondary by the large banks, at least in numeric terms, presumably because it reduces the chances for a single direction in business management. In the context of this sample, it is clearly not an alternative to the others but rather a complementary solution in the context of complex projects hinging on various strategic approaches.

On the basis of what we have seen thus far, the most interesting areas of technological development for the sample's banks seem to be personal finance and payment services. With reference to personal finance solutions, it is clear that various European banks have developed apps themselves or via partnerships. For example, ABN Amro has developed the Grip app which enables clients to monitor their expenses and plan their investments. DZ Bank has invested in fymio, a tool which enables clients to track their financial resources via apps and online. Lloyds Bank has improved current account opening experiences via mobile phones and created banking and insurance services app. UniCredit has invested in happymoney, a "financial wellbeing" app.

In the payments sector incumbents have pursued the objective of facilitating peer-to-peer (P2P) payments or payments at shops with various solutions being identified, sometimes in partnership with FinTech firms. For example, Credit Suisse set up a partnership with TWINT, while UniCredit was the first bank to activate Apple Pay in Italy and to use Alipay. Société Générale acquired the FinTech TagPay, which offers mobile phone payment services in Africa. In 2017, Standard Chartered was the first international bank to create a mobile wallet service in China.

Outside Europe, an especially innovative solution was introduced by The Bank of Tokyo—Mitsubishi UFJ (or MUFG), which created MUFG

Coin for payments via QR code and smartphone. Other interesting examples include JP Morgan Chase, which launched Chase Pay, an app which enables clients to make payments in actual shops and online with their smartphones. Moreover, JP Morgan Chase introduced a service (Zelle) which enables free money transfers to friends and family members which around 30 other large banks signed up to—in a consortium logic—in response to the initiative launched by PayPal via Venmo.

In the wealth management context, various of the sample banks (including European BBVA, BNP Paribas, Deutsche Bank, Santander, UBS and UniCredit and US Goldman Sachs and JP Morgan Chase) have set up partnerships or invested in FinTech to offer automised advisory services (robo advice). This area also encompasses specific solutions for the private customers. For example, ABN Amro set up Prospery, a FinTech offering digital asset management and expert coaching services. DZ Bank and Banco do Brasil have, on the other hand, developed specific digital wealth management solutions for retirement schemes.

With reference to corporate services a consortium launched by a range of European banks[4] for the we.trade platform, focusing on regulating European small and medium-sized enterprise's (SME's) international trading, is worthy of note with 13 European banks active in 14 different countries currently involved.

As we saw above, the in-house development strategies for banking groups field also encompasses the setting up or acquisition of online banks. Effectively, in the context of a wider digitalisation process affecting group structures and pre-existing production and distribution processes, six of the banks in our sample (five European—BBVA, BNP Paribas, Crédit Agricole, Groupe BPCE and UniCredit—and JP Morgan via its subsidiary Chase Bank) have opted to set up or buy up a native digital bank working exclusively online.[5]

This can be an especially rapid and effective solution, as compared to the time required for incumbent banks to enact a digital conversion process. Furthermore, the creation within a banking group of a native digital bank does not rule out the opportunity to work in parallel—as is effectively taking place—including in further digitalisation projects in other of the groups' distribution channels and specific processes and services. In this way, an in-house strategy can follow diverse time frames and respond variously to the needs of a differentiated clientele.[6]

Starting with the evidence emerging from this sample overall, we believe it to be important to assess the extent to which strategic approaches have been adopted primarily by the individual banks working on the digital development of their activities and to what degree of intensity. The results are summed up in Table 4.2 in which we have classified the banks into the following four categories:

Table 4.2 Prevailing digitalisation strategy and degree of diversification of European (bold) and non-European banks

Degree of diversification (according to areas of activity)	Main strategy adopted by the bank				Number of banks
	Shareholding-oriented	Partnership-oriented	In-house developer	Mixed strategy	
Low				BB	1
Medium-low	**BPCE, NAT**		MUFG	CS, **NOR**	5
Medium	**BBVA**	BNY	BC, **LL**	SC	5
Medium-high	**ABN, CZ, CM, DB, ING**		**DZ, ISP**	**BAR, CA, RABO, RBS, UBS**	12
High	CITI, GS, **SAN**			**BNP, HSBC**, JPM, MOSL, **SOGE, UC**	9
Number of banks	11	1	5	15	32

Key

European banks

ABN	ABN AMRO	**DB**	DEUTSCHE BANK	**LL**	LLOYDS BANKING GROUP
BBVA	BANCO BILBAO VIZCAYA ARGENTARIA	**DZ**	DZ BANK	**RABO**	RABOBANK
BAR	BARCLAYS	**BPCE**	GROUPE BPCE	**RBS**	ROYAL BANK OF SCOTLAND
BNP	BNP PARIBAS	**HSBC**	HSBC	**SAN**	SANTANDER
CZ	COMMERZBANK	**ING**	ING	**SOGE**	SOCIETE GENERALE
CA	CREDIT AGRICOLE	**ISP**	INTESA SANPAOLO	**SC**	STANDARD CHARTERED
CM	CREDIT MUTUEL	**NAT**	NATIXIS	**UBS**	UBS
CS	CREDIT SUISSE	**NOR**	NORDEA BANK	**UC**	UNICREDIT

Non-European banks

BB	BANCO DO BRASIL	CITI	CITIGROUP	MOSL	MORGAN STANLEY
BC	BANK OF CHINA	GS	GOLDMAN SACHS	MUFG	MUFG-BANK OF TOKYO
BNY	BANK OF NEW YORK MELLON	JPM	JP MORGAN CHASE		

- Shareholding-oriented: Banks which prefer a strategy based on acquisitions of FinTech or Tech firms for their digitalisation
- Partnership-oriented: Banks preferring to set up partnerships for the development of technologically advanced product and service development
- In-house developer: Banks primarily opting to develop from within, investing directly in their banks' IT structure or setting up firms in the group devoted to the development and/or provision of digitalised services, including native digital banks
- Mixed strategy: Banks which have adopted a mixed strategy, that is, a combination of the various strategic approaches listed above, without preferring one over the others.

Table 4.2 enables us to observe that the majority of banks adopt a plurality of strategic approaches concurrently (15 cases, 12 of which are European banks) or prefer to acquire FinTech and Tech companies (11 cases, 9 of which are European banks).

Furthermore, it is clear that an increasingly large proportion of banks (21 out of 32) has resorted to a multiplicity of financial activities or technological activities functional to the development of financial activities. This indicates that the main banks are acting on a wide array of fronts in order to identify digital development solutions suitable to their various business areas. This does not necessarily reflect a desire to pursue a progressive enlargement in the number of digitalised services offered, a fact which is credible given that it seems equally likely that, in individual cases, the banks may make conscious decisions to focus on areas relating to their core business and their main client segments.

It should also be underlined that whilst Table 4.2 shows that just one American bank (Bank of New York Mellon) has adopted a partnership-based strategy as its pre-eminent approach, effectively an analysis of our sample shows that all the main European and non-European banks have adopted partnership strategies, some very intense, with BigTech, FinTech and Tech firms.

It should also be added that for at least three of the five banks classified as in-house developers, internal development has not been their sole digital development approach. In particular, Bank of China is currently working with BigTech Tencent, while DZ Bank has invested in a FinTech firm working in payment services and, lastly, Italian Intesa Sanpaolo has declared an intention to activate a partnership within the blockchain technologies development area.

In the light of the great many innovation areas visible in our sample, it is worth highlighting the main lines of strategic development emerging from the documentation available to us in relation to the individual banks. This enables us to offer case studies relating to the previously cited EBA classification (EBA 2018) and contribute to an analysis of the ways in which individual banks are structuring their strategic approaches to digital transformation or digital disruption.

In the context of our sample, it is clear that the majority of the banks examined are undertaking a digital transformation trajectory based essentially on qualifying and diversifying their distribution channels.

At the same time only in a few cases does strategic planning seem to be at an advanced stage and based on innovation not only in distributional terms but also in the productive process. Consequently, the effective implementation of these digital disruption strategies is visible in a still limited number of banks as compared to the sample total considered. Moreover, it is not to be taken for granted that this approach will necessarily expand in view of the organisational difficulties which incumbent firms can encounter in implementing these strategies, which are primarily a matter of legacy and repercussions on human resources and the operational methods which these disruptive approaches bring with them.

An examination of the individual cases leads to further considerations. A first consideration is the fact that all the sample banks state that business digitalisation is a strategic goal and a challenge to be taken up. On closer examination, some of the incumbent banks have been making such declarations for some years now. A 2016 study by the International Data Corporation, a firm which specialises in market research, indicated that 96% of the credit institutions analysed mentioned having set a digitalisation strategy in motion. However, the same study found that 44% of these initiatives were exclusively front-office related, that is, mainly relating to the distributional channels (IDC 2016). More recently, a report by Ernst & Young has highlighted that a grand total of 85% of the banks interviewed cite this transformation process as a business priority in 2018 (EY 2018). This brings out the slow pace of implementation of this change process which we would attribute essentially to the complexity involved in productivity conversion within banks and in the complex structures of a group to an even greater extent.

With specific reference to our sample, the effective degree of digitalisation pursued by the individual banks varies widely. It is, in fact, clear that only some of the banks are genuinely rethinking their whole business approaches involving, for example, the digitalisation goals set out in strategic plans leading onto changes in manager payment systems coherent with effectively pursuing such objectives. Of the credit institutions based in Europe, for example, ING includes "driving digital transformation to improve customer experience and realise further efficiency gains" among its non-financial goals and ABN Amro refers to "transformation, innovation, digitalisation and sustainable growth" as the principles behind its executive body while Barclays cites achieving financial and non-financial objectives as determinant in executive pay and includes digitalisation in its non-financial goals. Other banks, on the other hand, cite wanting to digitalise business but are, at the moment, concentrating primarily on distribution channels and front-office (including Credit Suisse, Lloyds Bank and Nordea Bank and the non-European Banco do Brasil and Morgan Stanley).

On the basis of the evidence cited thus far, then, the re-organisation and digitalisation of distributional channels and multi-channel development is interesting. First and foremost we would like to emphasise that, whilst incumbent firms have, over the years, implemented increasingly rapid reductions in traditional branch numbers,[7] they have chosen strategically not to eliminate all physical contact with clients but rather to reformulate them in a more or less pronounced fashion. This aims to make branches less "traditional", more technological and functional and, at the same time, to reduce costs. An analysis of the sample shows that certain banks are implementing a policy of differentiation of their branch framework on the basis of the client segment which each specific branch is primarily devoted to. In this way, they are attempting to exploit technological opportunities to combine the cost reduction objective with greater service user friendliness from a client perspective, differentiating contact methods in line with their specific needs and a service provision characterised by variegated levels of standardisation or personalisation.

We are thus witnessing the development of entirely automatised branches which give clients access to basic and standardised services in an easy, ongoing way. This process affects retail clients, in particular, although certain banks have begun to implement digital channels dedicated to small and medium-size firms and professionals. These are assigned partially automatised branches with a number of consultants tasked with supporting clients in their more complex operations, as well as, branches with professionals providing services of greater added value to banks, primarily advisory services for wealth management and corporate banking operations.

Analysing individual cases gives us an insight into the specific way in which branch revision projects are carried out. Below are some of the main examples from our sample, to give an idea of the various degrees of implementation and innovation.

- Royal Bank of Scotland has implemented Cora, a digital assistant which uses artificial intelligence, and has brought technology experts into its branches (TechXpert) to support clients in the use of digital channels.
- Intesa Sanpaolo and UniCredit have planned to make certain branches fully automatic, conserving physical consultants in a limited number of branches dedicated to high added value services.
- Morgan Stanley reports a general goal of digitalising branches without, however, specifying client segmentation or differentiation in the degree of automation on the basis of the services and products offered.
- In addition to planning branch differentiation in line with client segment, MUFG-Bank of Tokyo has installed a humanoid at its Tokyo airport branch (Narita airport), which can supply base information for financial decisions in 19 languages.

In addition to reorganising and upgrading branches, the large world banks have, for some time, been paying special attention to diversification strategies in distribution channels and contact with clients. Multi-channels are held to be a strategic factor in attracting new clients (especially millennials), maintaining market shares or at least minimising loss of clients to FinTech and BigTech platforms, reducing costs and making the distribution process more efficient.

Analysing projects designed to develop a multi-channel approach and improve access to services, it emerges that the banks in our sample have activated apps with which clients can monitor their expenses, mobile websites and exclusively online products (online current accounts). Some of these projects have been developed exclusively in-house while others hinge on partnership agreements or buying up shares in FinTech and Tech firms. It is also notable that the development of these tools primarily targets retail clients but extended services or those developed specifically for corporate clients also exist.

In this respect too, we believe citing some of the main examples of European initiatives is of interest:

- ABN Amro has set up a lending platform called New10 which targets SMEs and can respond to lending applications in just 15 minutes for sums up to a maximum of 1 million euros.
- Crédit Agricole has come up with a solution based on blockchain technology, creating an automated supply chain in the corporate and investment banking sector. The service is mainly designed for clients wanting to obtain invoice pre-payment.
- DZ Bank has transformed its subsidiary VR Leasing into a digital supplier of lending solutions for small businesses and professionals.
- ING has introduced a virtual current account which enables firms' finance departments to manage cross-border cash flows between its subsidiaries in a unified way.
- Various banks, including Nordea, Deutsche Bank, HSBC, Natixis, Rabobank, Santander, Société Générale and UniCredit, have developed the previously cited we.trade platform to allow small and medium-sized businesses to negotiate with their partners across borders and also in foreign currency.
- Commerzbank has completed digitalisation of loan application and issuing to SMEs.
- UniCredit has launched a new portal for corporate clients together with virtual channels for retail.

It has to be noted that the setting up of digital platforms by the large international banks responds to the need to supply customers with innovative solutions and limit the effect of disintermediation generated by the creation of alternative financing channels to the banking one, which are the basis of the FinTech firms' success that gave birth to the new digital direct circuits.[8]

The incentives to innovation generated by the FinTech development find clear manifestation also in several specific initiatives of large banks which are experimenting with new instruments created within the digitalisation process. For instance, the recent set up of a Security Token Offering (STO) made by the group Société Générale, through the issue of a bond, entirely registered on the Ethereum blockchain system.[9] The initiative is particularly interesting not only because it is the first one to be implemented by a bank worldwide, but also—and most importantly—because of the importance of STO in the digitalisation process of financial markets. These, in fact, represent a more efficient process for the issue that enables to reduce time to market and improve scalability, automation, transparency, transferability and liquidability of securities.[10]

The many examples which have emerged here give an insight into the effort the large banks in our sample have been investing in taking on board technological evolutions and making them a driver of development. Moreover, the pervasive nature of the individual projects is extremely variegated, indicating an implementation even today which is still primarily centred on distribution channels and front-office. The efficacy of the individual projects can be grasped only on the basis of information—not made public—relating to the contributions such action can effectively have over time in terms of value generation for banks as well as the intensity and scale of use of the new channels and services by clients.

What emerges clearly from this analysis is that the main world incumbent firms are showing non-rapid time frames as regards the implementation of digitalisation development projects especially as compared with those of BigTech (Chap. 3). Considering the dimensions of the banks in our sample and the frequently especially large financial resources already invested to this purpose, we believe that this under dynamic approach can largely be explained by the difficulties facing large and complex corporate groups in implementing wide spectrum digital reconversion requiring focusing progressively on individual production and/or distribution areas within the multiplicity of companies belonging to a group.

The legacy theme seems especially important. The digital development underway effectively poses not solely the issue of investing in the acquisition of the most avant-garde technological solutions, but it also determines time frames and costs linked to the implementation of the new systems and, above all, to transferring the old systems which frequently generate interface problems and need to be replaced completely.[11]

The human resources theme should also not be underestimated. Such a drastic elimination of physical branches, digitalisation project development and the need for new skills bring out the problems banks have to face in managing resources and formulating training and education plans. To this it should be added that the regulatory and monitoring framework may have limited (including to different extents on the basis of the various national legal frameworks) both the options available to the banks strategically and operationally and the potential for reducing compliance burdens following logics similar to those experienced in the same operational contexts by new unregulated financial operators. The banks can effectively come up against constraints both in adopting outsourcing solutions and in drawing regulatory advantages via recourse to unbundling.

As the Basel Committee highlighted, "as fintech evolves, scope exists for greater outsourcing of bank operations, which would then potentially take place outside a supervised environment". However, this same Committee has underlined that control over service outsourcing choices is implemented only in some legal frameworks and only via certain types of regulated financial intermediaries (BIS-BCBS 2018). Thus on the basis of the current European regulations, even in cases in which banks proceed to outsourcing choices, the risk and responsibility for the activities outsourced remain theirs.[12] This is not the case in other contexts which thus offer banks the opportunity to outsource specific activities to FinTech firms or identify further solutions to reduce legal compliance burdens (Bofondi and Gobbi 2017).

In perspective, then, the survival of wide-ranging legal dishomogeneity across geographical areas and types of financial operators, and any intensification of competition relating to BigTech, may prompt the large international banks to enact different strategic choices from the past, in terms of geographical and operational positioning and similar to those enacted to date by FinTech and BigTech firms.

4.3   The Options for Smaller Banks: The Partnership Option

For smaller banks too, implementing business digitalisation is a priority, above all in consideration of the fact that their main target customer is retail, on which the FinTech development mainly rely on. In the current market scenario, the smaller banks are facing a twofold challenge. On one hand, these need to identify solutions which enable them to keep up with new and old competitors and the demands of a clientele which is looking for a more digital banking experience. On the other, the financial resources available to them are evidently smaller than those of the larger banks and their technology is not generally advanced, which makes in-house, autonomous development of digital innovation an especially challenging matter.

Observing the operational status quo highlights that, to date, many smaller banks, and those working in operational and market contexts less subject to competitive pressure, are adopting a wait-and-see type approach as regards FinTech. This may relate to the complexity of the theme or a limited awareness of the impact which FinTech may actually have on the banking market and, above all, client preferences.[13]

It should be noted that change can come gradually, in a process involving increasing the efficiency of the structure to be set up via:

- a rationalisation of the network of branches which has constituted the privileged point of contact with clients and with the traditional business model of smaller banks;
- a progressive development of base digital services[14] in order to better satisfy new client demands, especially from the young.

An aspect which is frequently pointed to as a critical issue for the smaller banks is their starting technological level. It has, in fact, been highlighted that a bank starting from a higher technological level can achieve a higher level of digitalisation more easily, while an intermediary operating with an entirely traditional model will first have to implement digitalisation in the most elementary sectors and processes before launching (if they decide to do so) the development of a more sophisticated model (PWC 2018). However, this progressive trajectory could turn out to be well-suited to gradual changes in demand by clients for increasingly digitalised services.[15] Furthermore, small banks can be more flexible and capable of adapting over time as they do not face the problems linked to a complex system legacy which we looked at above for the large banks.

We would argue that the aspect which may turn out to be truly critical is the time frames involved in a gradual process which may be too long, as compared to FinTech's competitive dynamics.[16] We have, in fact, seen that these dynamics are especially powerful in markets—such as the European market, above all that of continental Europe—in which FinTech has developed more recently. International experiences indicate that many banking systems have witnessed a process of fusion or even aggregation into group structures which have enabled firms to take advantage of economies of scale and create more favourable conditions for the implementation of centralised investments, supporting the strategic development of the group's individual banks. The outcome of processes of this sort has been especially evident for several years now, at a European level, in co-operative credit banks which have generated banks such as Crédit Agricole, Groupe BPCE and Rabobank—now some of the largest international players (Sect. 4.2).[17]

Internationally, small to medium-sized banks are also experimenting with other digitalisation development solutions (primarily partnership agreements with FinTech firms, as well as consortia and joint ventures) which can facilitate firms in their attempts to overcome the technological gap, improve client relations and pursue a more rapid achievement of their business model redefinition goals, as compared to what is possible on an in-house basis alone.

In a recent study, Hornuf et al. (2018) analysed the relation between FinTech firms and a sample of international banks and showed that less profitable banks have a greater propensity to initiate partnerships with lots of FinTechs, probably as a result of the competitive pressures on their business models. Faced with limited investment potential, the banks are in any case obliged to innovate to conserve their market shares and not fall behind.

Numerous examples of partnership between FinTechs and banks or other financial intermediaries have already been supplied in Sect. 2.3 and offer food for thought in an evaluation of the potential offered by such solutions. Here, we would like to add an example from Italy where FinTech developed later than other European countries but is showing rapid growth. In particular, the initiative developed in 2016, by ICCREA Banca, which invested in Ventis (an e-commerce portal), to foster the visibility and online sales of its corporate clients, and in Satispay (FinTech firm active in digital payments) to develop complementary payment services and reach a young customer base oriented towards the use of advanced digital tools. The project has generated advantages for mutual banks too which signed up to the project and were able to offer these opportunities to their own retail clients (individuals and SMEs).

As regards overseas markets the experience of the American community banks who have resorted widely to partnerships with FinTech firms, especially for the development of lending services, is worthy of note. In this respect, American Bankers Association (ABA 2018) indicates that two main partnership models are currently being used in which a bank and its partner can offer co-branding products for the purposes of selecting the product most suitable to their clients, drawing on banking intermediary and FinTech services. Specifically, the two approaches are as follows:

- Outbound referrals: In this case banks have first contact with clients and having evaluated their needs, pass them on to their FinTech partners who enter into contracts with clients and undersign their loans. Specifically, banks pass on potential FinTech borrowers where clients' demands or risk profiles are not compatible with banks' credit policies.

- Inbound referrals: In this case clients apply to FinTech firms which originate a loan. In the event that the loan granted and the client have a risk profile coherent with those required by the bank partner, FinTech firms may transfer the loan to the bank.

This solution is used on a voluntary basis in other markets, too. By contrast, in the UK a "bank referral scheme" has been formulated which obliges larger banks to report subjects that they have decided not to lend to, to FinTechs.[18] This law—formulated to increase the potential for recourse to financial resources by clients not funded by the large banks—facilitates the smaller banks in taking advantage of their opportunities. Partnerships with FinTech firms effectively enable a division of labour to be delineated between financial operators targeting retail clients. Furthermore, such agreements enable smaller banks, on one hand, to position themselves as regards their clients of choice in a way which is coherent with the new market context and, on the other, to fill the technological gap, identifying forms of partnership with better-equipped players from this perspective.

4.4   DIGITAL NATIVE BANKS: BUSINESS MODEL INNOVATION AND FLEXIBILITY

A further phenomenon which has emerged in the new financial activities digitalisation context is the creation of an especially large number of native digital banks. A first categorisation of this type of bank can be supplied by using the definition put forward in the BIS-BCBS (2018) report which called these new operators "challenger banks" and clarified that they are newly formed digital natives capable of supplying improved customer experiences and responding more effectively to clients' changing needs. The report highlighted, furthermore, that these new operators are implementing a banking model which is no longer branch centred, that is, linked to the physical presence of a branch in an area, but exclusively technologically based, enabling such banks to reach clients via various channels anywhere and anytime.

This definition does not seem to distinguish such banks from online banks which are certainly not new and have already been much experimented with internationally. For example, in 1991, ING created an exclusively online bank in-house, ING Direct. Technology has always characterised the British First Direct, too, founded in 1989 and controlled by HSBC which began working as a telephone bank and then went online in the year 2000. In 1999, WeBank was set up in Italy and works within Gruppo Banco BPM S.p.A. offering exclusively online banking and trading services and products. As non-European examples, we cite Japanese Sony Bank, set up as an internet-specialised bank in 2001, within the Sony group via its subsidiary Sony Financial, an example of a bank deriving from an industry.

In analyses of FinTech firms, the banks referred to here are frequently classified as incumbent banks and thus on a par with traditional banks rather than "new generation" digital banks because these latter have more advanced technology and propose different business and client relations approaches.[19]

Further light can be thrown on these initial observations by an analysis of new generation digital native banks and their specific features as compared to incumbent firms in order to gain an insight into how the business model with which banking can potentially be done is changing. To this end, we have identified a great many examples of digital native banks set up in recent years and shown, in Table 4.3, the 22 cases in which the standardised information required for our analysis is available. It also seemed opportune to encompass European and non-European native digital banks in the sample, for compare and contrast purposes. Specifically, Table 4.3 shows 13 European and 9 non-European banks.

By identifying the main shareholders we were able to distinguish between independent banks (panel A) and those operating within banking groups (panel B) or BigTech groups (panel C). This seemed opportune not simply in order to take account of the variety of circumstances now visible on the market but also because the motives behind the setting up of a challenger bank can vary according to who sets it up. An analysis of the sample's banks made it possible to draw certain interesting conclusions, first and foremost as regards their specific features as compared to incumbent banks.

The new generation online digital banks benefit from the chance to emerge and develop in a favourable technological environment because they adopt the most recent technology and make it immediately operational via an innovative approach. This is a fundamental difference with the incumbent banks whether traditional or old generation online banks. In fact, as we have seen, incumbent banks face a large and burdensome upgrading task or, more frequently, convert their information and communications technology (ICT) systems in order to take on board the most recent technological innovations. Certainly, the work required by an old generation online bank is more limited than that required by a traditional

Table 4.3 Selected examples of digital native banks with their main features

No.	Digital native banks	Date of founding	Nation (European countries in bold)	Products offered
Panel A: Independents				
1	**Atom bank**	2014	**UK**	Deposits and mortgages
2	**Bunq**	2015	**Netherlands**	Deposits, payment cards and money transfers It also offers an electronic piggy bank service
3	**Chime**	2013	USA	Visa debit card, automatic savings programme, no fees, real-time alerts and daily balance updates. Offers cashback rewards on purchases, and 1.75% on savings
4	**Monzo**	2015	**UK**	Real-time breakdown of spending habits, quick mobile money transfers, integration with other day-to-day tech like Uber
5	**N26**	2013	**Germany**	Account deposits, loans, insurance and B2B accounts
6	**Nubank**	2013	Brazil	Current accounts, payment cards and reward programmes with partners
7	**Revolut**	2013	**UK**	Insurance, crypto currencies accounts, B2B accounts
8	**solarisBank**	2016	**Germany**	Account deposits, payment services
9	**Starling Bank**	2014	**UK**	Mobile-only account deposits, insurance and B2B account
10	**Varo Money**	2015	USA	Current account, deposits, savings account and personal loans
11	**Younited Credit**	2008	**France**	Personal loans

(*continued*)

Table 4.3 (continued)

No.	Digital native banks	Date of founding	Nation (European countries in bold)	Products offered	Parent company
Panel B: Incumbent subsidiaries					
12	**CBD Now**	2016	UAE	Online account opening in 5 minutes, with a debit card hand-delivered within 24 hours	Commercial Bank of Dubai
13	**CheBanca!**	2008	**Italy**	Current accounts, insurance policies and investment services including via robo advice	Mediobanca
14	**Fidor**	2009	**Germany**	A current account that pays interest rates influenced by Facebook likes, and an active "Smart Community" platform for discussing financial matters	Set up independently and bought up in 2017 by Groupe BPCE
15	**Eko**	2017	**France**	Current accounts and payment cards	Crédit Agricole
16	**Finn**	2017	USA	Checking and savings tied to a prepaid debit card. Customers can open an account, make deposits, issue checks, track spending and set up savings plans on the phone. Users can rate transactions	Chase (subsidiary of JP Morgan Chase)
17	**Hello Bank**	2013	**Belgium**	One of the largest and most sophisticated digital banks in Europe, offering current account, insurance, loans, savings and brokerages services	BNP Paribas
18	**Simple**	2009	USA	Current accounts, payment cards and spending check services	Set up independently and bought up in 2014 by the BBVA Group

(*continued*)

Table 4.3 (continued)

No.	Digital native banks	Date of founding	Nation (European countries in bold)	Products offered	Parent company
19	**Widiba**	2013	**Italy**	Diversified banking services including: current accounts, savings accounts, cards and payments, trading and investment services and loans	Monte dei Paschi di Siena

No.	Digital native banks	Date of founding	Nation	Products offered	Parent company
Panel C: BigTech subsidiaries					
20	**Ant Financial**	2014	China	Payment services, lending to small businesses, consumer credit, own and partner investment funds:	Alibaba
21	**MYbank**	2014	China	Online banking services	Alibaba (via Ant Financial)
22	**WeBank**	2015	China	Retail loans and partner financial services	Tencent

Source: Authors' elaboration of data from bank, BigTech and incumbent firm websites and from https://thefinancialbrand.com/69560/25-direct-online-digital-banks/

bank or complex group and can thus allow for a more rapid technological upgrade and market consolidation.[20] However, the change must be managed in an ICT framework in dialogue with its parent company also for the purposes of benefiting from synergies within the group which enable the services offered to be extended and client relations to be consolidated, both of which mark out newly founded native digital banks from their rivals.

A second element closely related to the technological element emerges from a consideration that, in various cases, the priority goal of the native digital banks is speed and immediate responses to client's financial demands. For example, CBD Now (Table 4.3, panel B) opens current accounts online in just 5 minutes and sends clients cash cards within 24 hours. British Monzo (Table 4.3, panel A) supplies real-time details on spending habits using current account data allowing for rapid money transfers and additional commonly used services such as Uber.

A further aspect which emerges is that relating to marketing approach. The native digital banks operate via especially straightforward and appealing websites and interfaces including with younger client groups. Sites are minimalist in contents and forms, probably in order to optimise mobile phone and tablet viewing. Only some of the sites have menus giving access to lists of products offered and use of the site by non-clients is limited. In most cases, sites are packed with images and have limited amounts of text. Legal information (licences from regulatory bodies, company data, etc.) are collected into specific pages and presented informally.[21]

In business model terms all the native digital banks in our sample (both European and non-European) primarily offer current account deposits, payment services and money transfers. Lending services are less frequent and thus exposure to credit or counterparty risks is limited (Table 4.3). The primary activity of these native digital banks—on a par with non-banking FinTech firms—thus determines profits, centring around commission rather than interest margins. This model makes these banks especially flexible in the face of any service provision repositioning which may be required and lowers their need for capital resources in the light of the limited financial risks they are exposed to. These aspects can be important advantages from the point of view of their ability to compete in a market dominated by large international players.

Looking in further depth at the individual panels shown in Table 4.3, however, highlights certain further specific features. In particular the new independent digital banks (panel A) focus more on "base" products (current accounts and payments) while the other digital banks (panels B and C) set up within banking or industrial groups (both before and after the FinTech wave) offer a more diversified range of services (current accounts complete with all functions, loan and funding services, wealth management products and insurance).

In the light of this, it seems plausible that setting up independent native digital banks (panel A) is essentially a matter of direct current account management in order to offer clients payment and money transfer services and avoid depending on other banks for their current accounts. As regards the other native digital banks (panels B and C) it is clear that their group allegiance enables them to take advantage of productive synergies in order to attract the widest range of clients. More specifically the native digital banks set up by the BigTechs (panel C) are "captive" banks designed to fulfil the needs of the industrial parent company's clients and benefit from joint working with the group's other financial companies or partnerships to extend the range of services offered to clients. The native digital banks incorporated into banking groups (panel B) can certainly exploit synergies with other firms within the group but these are presumably assigned the task of market action consisting of responding effectively to the needs of specific client groups not covered by the other firms in a banking group or for which the use of online channels is preferred. In other words, the presence of a native digital bank within a banking group can enable reference client groups to be segmented, entrusting the retail target group to the online bank to whom a sufficiently standardised range of services can be offered at reduced cost thanks to technological solutions which facilitate production and provision.

Taking a closer look at the individual panels in Table 4.3 highlights further specific features of the various types of challenger bank. Digital native banks independent of banking groups or industrial/technology groups (panel A) are a feature of the FinTech phenomenon, that is, they are born from a desire to form innovative operators capable of taking advantage of the most recent technologies to respond rapidly, effectively and cheaply to clients' needs. This specific category of FinTech firms, with their banking licences, makes use of an especially favourable competitive milieu for online bank entry and has shown an ability to attract new clients on the basis of advanced technologies which enable them to offer services especially cost effectively above all in the money transfer and payment contexts.

Of the 11 independent banks set up over the last decade in various markets encompassed by our sample, 8 are in Europe, 2 in the USA and 1 in Brazil (Table 4.3, panel A). On the operational level, we have already highlighted that the native digital banks primarily offer current accounts and payment services. We can add that, to this end, in some cases, they enter into partnerships with consolidated credit card circuits and, furthermore, to attract clients they often propose a free or low-cost basic service which encompasses a current account and a credit card.

It has also emerged that the only in certain specific cases do the activities of the native digital banks also encompass deposit collection for credit purposes which is the distinctive characteristic of banks as compared to other credit institutions, payment institutions and other financial intermediaries.[22] Furthermore, credit services are generally developed adopting an "originate to distribute" model widely used in the FinTech lending environment (Chap. 2). An example of this is French Younited credit which works in the European market, offering personal loans which are then securitised and positioned via investment funds reserved to professional investors (Table 4.3, panel A).

This movement away from a traditional banking activity model is even more evident if a further case is shown in Table 4.3 (panel A) is considered, that is, Revolut, a bank which offers business-to-business (B2B) accounts, crypto currencies accounts and insurance services and was granted a banking licence in Europe in December 2018.[23] This FinTech firm can thus extend the range of products offered its clients, offering current account deposits and loans in the milieu reserved to banks. The native digital banks thus offer products such as deposits in crypto currencies which are not present in traditional circuits at present.

With reference to the independent native digital banks, further considerations relating to their shareholding structure can be formulated. It should, in fact, be highlighted that, when they are set up, their shareholders include other non-financial firms or venture capital and private equity funds. In some cases the development of these challenger banks has been made possible also by the intervention of incumbent banks who have invested directly in them, acquiring shares in their capital,[24] or indirectly by their shareholders investing in venture capital funds. The former model was followed by Crédit Mutuel Arkea, which bought shares in French Younited Credit whilst the latter was used by BBVA, one of the venture capital fund investor shareholders in Atom bank.

It can also be highlighted that, in some cases, the interest of the incumbent banks has taken the form of buying up a native digital bank and thus its incorporation into a banking group (Table 4.3, panel B). A first example of this is American bank Simple, which offers current accounts and payment tools and services and gives its clients easy access to spending control functions via app. This bank was set up independently in 2009 and became part of the BBVA group in 2014. A second example is German Fidor, born in 2009 as an online independent bank[25] and bought up by French Groupe BPCE in 2017. The Fidor example is especially interesting because Groupe BPCE's interest was triggered by the success of a bank which links banking services to social media. Fidor's interest rates to individual savers are affected by the number of "likes" they get on their Facebook page and their participation in the bank's community.

The other native digital banks shown in panel B in Table 4.3 were set up by incumbent banks within their own groups and it is noticeable that this solution has intensified in more recent years and affects many geographical areas. As we have seen, the strategic decision to buy or set up a challenger bank can respond to a range of perceived bank needs, essentially related to a desire to fill the technological gap as rapidly as possible and task these online banks with responding to the needs of more digitally evolved clients, possibly in a client segmentation logic which can assign retail clients not served by the other firms in the group to challenger banks.

To this, we can add that the way in which the digitalisation solutions used by banking groups are implemented is still evolving as can be seen, for example, by UniCredit. In 2018, this Italian bank launched the Buddybank service which is accessed exclusively via iPhone. Buddybank is thus not a native digital bank with its own banking licence distinct from that of the UniCredit parent company. It is rather a solution which UniCredit calls "a conversational bank service" which enables it to work globally with its clients rather than simply selling them banking or financial services.[26] This enables UniCredit to offer its products also via this new digital channel (an app), including the current account Buddybank. This generates a sort of "white labelling" mechanism as the services have a specific brand, whilst in this case, the producer is the same parent group bank which set up the Buddybank service.

At last, Table 4.3's panel C lists native digital banks set up by the Chinese BigTech firms previously analysed in the course of this work (Chap. 3). We will thus simply highlight that these differ from other challenger banks in that their goal is to work alongside payment platforms (both online and offline) or other digital channels used by the parent company and contribute to its financial services as compared to Tencent and Alibaba's core business. In fact, these native digital banks supply payment services and loans to e-commerce platforms (Alibaba) and message app (Tencent) users. Furthermore, WeBank and Ant Financial were able to exploit the internet to work with clients living in areas not covered by traditional credit institution banking services, accessing a user basin with no previous access to banking. To this, it should be added that clients can, if they like, access not only the services of this same bank through the online banks of these two BigTech firms but also more complex services from other incumbent banks, thanks to partnerships activated by these BigTechs.

Notes

1. The database originated partly from Tanda (2018) but has been further extended, updated and supplemented. The information relating to individual sample banks' digital development projects was updated from their company websites, financial statements and financial reports, shareholder presentations and road shows, press releases and industrial plans, where these are publicly available. For shareholding and partnership data, the S&P Capital IQ database was also used.

2. A list of the banks included in the sample is shown in Table 4.2. Note that our specific interest in the European system prompted us to include the main European banking groups and other smaller entities in our sample. This decision was not bank size considerations based but also took account of the characteristics of the European banking system and the innovation level of certain projects launched by a number of large banks working internationally. Certain of the non-European principal banks have also been included to represent the state of the art in projects launched in various markets and areas, including the USA, Brazil, China and Japan.

3. As defined by BIS, "RegTech is an application or platform which makes regulatory compliance more efficient through automated processes and lowers the costs of compliance. RegTech focuses on technologies that facilitate the delivery of regulatory requirements more efficiently and effectively" (Das 2019, p. 4).

4. Initially developed by Deutsche Bank, HSBC, KBC, Natixis, Rabobank and Société Générale, UniCredit, later joined by Nordea and Santander and finally by CaixaBank, Erste Group, Eurobank and UBS.

5. For further consideration of the native digital banks, see Sect. 4.3.

6. In perspective, we believe, the European Commission (2018) European Crowdfunding Service Providers regulation proposal referred to above may clear the way for new European banking group choices relating to the creation (on their own or in partnership with FinTech firms or other banks) of online platforms alongside other service provision channels. In fact this solution may respond to management logic as regards the various client segments and differing risk exposure linked to financial activities: direct exposure in the case of bank loans and externalisation of the risks with reference to the group's marketplace activities as regards specific client segments.

7. On the international bank transition process towards a branchless model, see Gomber et al. (2017).

8. The international favour in the development of FinTech finds one of its main motivations in the will to increment the availability of multiple financing channels (OECD 2018). One of the most recent examples of the effects of disintermediation of banks activated by FinTech is the decision by the European Investment Bank (EIB) to finance SMEs not only through the traditional banking channel, but also rather through partner FinTech platforms. In detail, in April 2019, the EIB allowed 100 million euros to finance German and Dutch SMEs through Funding Circle, a British P2P lending platform (EIB 2019). The partnership between EIB and Funding Circle dates back to 2016, when a similar operation to the favour of UK SMEs took place (EIB 2016).

9. More in detail, Société Générale SFH, part of the French banking group, issued a guarantee bond loan ("obligations de financement de l'habitat" or "OFH") for a countervalue of 100 million euros. The STO was entirely underwritten by the holding Société Générale and the security token obtained an evaluation of Aaa and AAA respectively, by Moody's and Fitch agencies. The bank states the pilot project was launched by Société Générale and Société Générale FORGE, one of the 60 start-ups set up internally via the project "Internal Startup Call". The project fosters the internal management to experiment with FinTech innovations to create disruptive solutions. In the above examples, blockchain was involved (see https://www.societegenerale.com/fr/node/51522).

10. It is the case to recall that security tokens are not crypto assets or token related to an ICO (Initial Coin Offering). Similar to traditional financial instruments (stocks, bonds, shares of funds, etc.), security tokens have a monetary value and can be traded. The differency to other instruments is that security tokens are originated by smart contracts and that the ownership of the instrument is confirmed by a blockchain transaction. The smart contract is an informatic protocol that facilitates the digitalisation, verification and management of a negotiation or a contract. It can, hence, allow the execution of transaction that is believed credible (because not changeable and tracked) without the intervention of third party.

11. Sperimborgo (2016) has highlighted that the strategies adopted by the banks do not always turn out to be effective or profitable. He also carries out an analysis, not limited to IT elements alone, of the organisational and management processes which should inspire bank business model reformulation and the complex operational implementation which becomes necessary if financial investments are to be profitable and generate value.

12. An especially delicate issue relates to cloud computing or outsourcing data and information management services to an outside and unregulated body which constitute a strategic financial resource. The European banks are subject to especially stringent regulations in this matter (BIS-BCBS 2018, Appendix 2), in that the regulatory authorities and the Committee of European Banking Supervisors have drawn up rules designed to limit the operational risks deriving from outsourcing to providers outside the EU. Furthermore EU legislation requires cloud computing to conform to laws relating to personal data protection and security (General Data Protection Regulation or GDPR). Limited recourse by the European banks to cloud computing, which potentially constitutes a significant saving in terms of data conservation and elaboration, is to be explained by this regulatory framework and by the desire to safeguard such information assets in consideration of the fact that "*on the infrastructure side, bigtech firms are already dominant providers of cloud services worldwide*" (BIS-BCBS 2018).

13. Where, on the other hand, awareness of the market context does exist, alongside a capacity for governance and managerial skills with which to conduct a digital development trajectory, small to medium-sized banks can develop initiatives in the technological milieu and digital ecosystem (such as workshops, incubators, etc.) which facilitate the identification of operational solutions in-house and/or in partnership. An example in the Italian context is Banca Sella, which has set up a Fintech district (www.fintechdistrict.com/) and generated a great many joint working methods with FinTech firms.

14. In-house solutions which can be made use of by a small bank are the least costly and most straightforward, such as digital channel creation and apps with which clients can access current accounts and services.

15. As Carbò-Valverde et al. have noted (2018), this progressive development, which leads from more elementary to more sophisticated processes and products, is coherent with adoption time frames by clients of banks for digitalised banking and financial services. In particular, the study shows that clients' first digital service is access to their current account telematically and they only later move on to digital channels for transfers using mobile banking or a virtual channel with which to communicate with banks.

16. A survey by the American Bankers Association (ABA 2018) of around 200 banks (70% of which were community banks) showed that the banks interviewed had already implemented an online or digital channel for loans (in 82% of cases) and consumer credit (58%) but had great room for improvement in the use of technology to increase volumes and reduce costs, thus improving efficiency.

17. In other European countries, including Italy, the number of smaller banks is still today very high. In the specific Italian case, it is made up primarily of mutual banks which, on the basis of the 2017 law reform, are obliged to aggregate into group structures. Banca d'Italia has repeatedly emphasised the need to speed up the launch of these co-operative groups in consideration of the weakness of the mutual banks business model, centred on traditional service provision and the prevalence of traditional banking branches which are further undermined by banking market change prospects, strongly affected by growing digitalisation and the resulting competitive pressures in local markets, too (Barbagallo 2018).

18. The Small and Medium Sized Business (Credit Information) Regulations came into force in the UK on 1 April 2016 and enforced an obligation for the larger intermediaries to make available their credit information regarding SMEs to FinTechs (Bofondi 2017).

19. This can effectively be clarified citing the interesting account of Takeda (2018) on Sony Bank: "*Sony Bank was established in 2001 as an Internet-specialized bank. While ensuring fair business practices, the Bank has*

expanded its business scale successfully by redefining traditional financial services. We are cautious about the overwhelming speed of service development and cost competitiveness of digital companies, like German-based Fidor Bank, that specialize in back-end services by forming alliances with front-end service providers. Seventeen years after its establishment, Sony Bank is often regarded in the same way as traditional financial institutions. However, the Internet consistently remains our core business area. Sony Bank, which has offered basic banking services, such as housing loans, foreign currency deposits, and investment trusts in the digital world can take the financial reform and market expansion by new digital entrants as an opportunity for further growth. With the advancement of open banking such as API, new value creation is expected to accelerate through alliances with external companies, allowing unbundling and white labelling (The 'white labelling' is a mechanism to incorporate financial products developed by one company into another company's financial services or to provide them to customers under the brand name of another company. Customers purchase products or services trusting the brand name of the distributor without knowing the manufacturer)".

20. For example, ING Direct is now continuing with its digital development strategy and claims to be a digital banking market leader: digital channels represent 98% of its individual client contacts (ING, Annual Report 2018). Sony Bank offers foreign currency deposits, investment funds and loans and, as we have seen, is proceeding to rework its digital development strategies.

21. For example, British Atom bank's website has its legal notices on a page called the "legal bits". Another example is indications relating to the number of licences granted by regulatory bodies which, in the case of the UK native and digital banks, is always shown in small script at the bottom of the page.

22. In the EU context banks are defined by Capital Requirements Regulation (CRR) (Art. 4, Section 1, point 1) "'credit institution' means an undertaking the business of which is to take deposits or other repayable funds from the public and to grant credits for its own account". Note, moreover, that the guidelines for the granting of a banking licence to "FinTech credit institutions" in the EU published by European Central Bank (ECB 2018) specify that the two activities must both be developed at the outset of business or within a period held to be acceptable by regulatory bodies (12 months). This underlines a distance from native digital banks which to date work on the market using a business model which differs, sometimes significantly, from this definition of banking activities.

23. On its own site, in early 2019, the firm claimed to have begun a series of tests for the purposes of becoming fully operational as a bank in the months following on from its being granted a banking licence (blog.revolut.com).

24. The entity of this shareholding is difficult to estimate and track as the process and sums involved in incumbent bank investment in independent digital native banks are not always publicly reported.

25. The bank is part of Fidor Group, together with a firm which develops technological solutions for online banks and digital banking services (www. fidor.de/about-fidor/about-us).
26. See www.buddybank.com/it/faq/.

References

ABA (American Bankers Association). (2018). *The state of digital lending.*

Barbagallo, C. (2018, October 9). *La riforma delle Banche di Credito Cooperativo: presupposti e obiettivi [The reform of the Cooperative Credit Banks: Assumptions and objectives].* Speech by the Director General for Financial Supervision and Regulation, Bank of Italy at the University of Naples "Parthenope".

BIS-BCBS. (2018, February). *Sound practices. Implications of fintech developments for banks and bank supervisors.* Basel Committee on Banking Supervision—BIS. Retrieved March 27, 2019, from https://www.bis.org/bcbs/publ/d431.pdf.

Bofondi, M. (2017). *Lending-based crowdfunding: Opportunities and risks.* Banca d'Italia Occasional Papers—Questioni di Economia e Finanza, n. 375/2017.

Bofondi, M., & Gobbi, G. (2017). The big promise of Fintech. *European Economy, 2,* 107–119.

Carbò-Valverde, F., Cuadro-Solas, P. J., & Rodríguez-Fernández, F. (2018). *How do bank customers go digital? A random forest approach.* Retrieved March 27, 2019, from https://papers.ssrn.com/sol3/papers.cfm?abstract_id=3195286.

Das, S. (2019, March 25). *Opportunities and challenges of FinTech.* Keynote address by Mr Shaktikanta Das, Governor of the Reserve Bank of India, at FinTech Conclave 2019, organized by NITI Aayog, New Delhi.

EBA. (2018, July 3). *EBA report on the impact of Fintech on incumbent credit institutions' business models.*

ECB. (2018, March). *Guide to assessments of fintech credit institution licence applications.*

EIB. (2016, June 20). *United Kingdom: EIB and Funding Circle announce groundbreaking £100 million investment into small businesses.* Retrieved April 28, 2019, from https://www.eib.org/en/press/all/2016-154-eib-and-funding-circle-announce-groundbreaking-pound100-million-investment-into-uk-small-businesses.htm.

EIB. (2019, April 17). *Germany/Netherlands: Investment plan—EIB lends EUR 100 million to small businesses through Funding Circle platform.* Retrieved April 28, 2019, from https://www.eib.org/fr/press/all/2019-104-ein-lends-eur-100m-to-small-businesses-through-funding-circle-platform.

European Commission. (2018, March 8). *Proposal for a regulation of the European Parliament and of the council on European Crowdfunding Service Providers (ECSP) for business.* COM(2018) 113 final, 2018/0048 (COD), Brussels.

EY (Ernst & Young Global Limited). (2018). *Global banking outlook 2018—Pivoting toward an innovation-led strategy.* Retrieved from ey.com/bankinginnovation.

Gomber, P., Kauffman, R. J., Parker, C., & Weber, B. W. (2017). *On the Fintech revolution: Interpreting the forces of innovation, disruption and transformation in financial services.* Retrieved March 27, 2019, from https://ssrn.com/abstract=3190052.

Hornuf, L., Klus, M. F., Lohwasser, T. S., & Schwienbacher, A. (2018, July). *How do banks interact with Fintechs? Forms of alliances and their impact on bank value.* Cesifo working paper, 7170. ISSN 2364-1428.

IDC. (2016). *The digital-ready bank. How ready are European banks for a digital world.* IDC Financial Insights white paper.

ING. (2018). *Annual report.* Retrieved March 31, 2019, from https://www.ing.com/Investor-relations/Financial-Reports/Annual-reports.htm.

OECD. (2018, February 22–23). *Enhancing SME access to diversified financing instruments.* Discussion paper. Mexico City, SME Ministerial Confer.

PWC. (2018). *3 models for banks to start a digital transformation.* Retrieved March 27, 2019, from https://blog.pwc.lu/3-models-banks-start-digital-transformation/.

Sperimborgo, S. (2016). *Banche e innovazione tecnologica. Come avere successo nella tempesta perfetta della rivoluzione digitale [Banks and technological innovation. How to succeed in the perfect storm of the digital revolution].* Bancaria, n. 12.

Takeda, K. (2018, July 11). Sony bank: Open banking accelerates new business value creation. *Fujitsu Journal.* Retrieved March 27, 2019, from https://journal.jp.fujitsu.com/en/.

Tanda, A. (2018). *The digitalization of foreign banks, in AIBE-Consilia (2018), Foreign banks and financial intermediaries in Italy.* The support to Italian economy in 2017. Retrieved March 27, 2019, from https://www.aibe.it/pubblicazioni/attivita-banche-estere/.

CHAPTER 5

The Regulatory Framework and Initiatives

Abstract FinTech activities often take place within an unregulated space or are subject to non-homogeneous regulatory frameworks. After a prevalent approach of "wait-and-see" by regulators, followed by an intense (still ongoing) debate on the opportunity to regulate, national authorities and international regulatory bodies have started to design regulatory provisions. The main aims are to eliminate the space for regulatory arbitrage and ensure the financial markets greater stability and resilience, as well as to provide customers and investors with a higher degree of protection. Co-operation between authorities in this area of regulation is key to the success of the new provisions, given the pervasiveness and innovative features of FinTech. This chapter reviews the regulatory approaches adopted so far and describes the main regulatory actions taken at the European level.

Keywords Level playing field • Regulatory arbitrage • Banking licence • Innovation hub • Regulatory sandbox

5.1   FinTech Regulatory State-of-the-Art

In the course of this work, it has emerged that FinTech firms work on an uneven regulatory playing field in which similar or equivalent activities are subject to diverse legal frameworks and sometimes to none at all. Some FinTech firms were set up to exploit gaps in relation to some financial

© The Author(s) 2019
A. Tanda, C.-M. Schena, *FinTech, BigTech and Banks*, Palgrave Macmillan Studies in Banking and Financial Institutions,
https://doi.org/10.1007/978-3-030-22426-4_5

activities not reserved to financial intermediaries, such as peer-to-peer lending, for example (Zetzsche et al. 2017). In 2017, the European Banking Authority reported that over 30% of the FinTech firms doing business in Europe are subject to no regulatory regimes whatsoever (EBA 2017).

The fragmentation of the phenomenon and the various degrees of FinTech development shown in the various countries have contributed powerfully to the current co-existence of a range of regulatory frameworks (BIS-BCBS 2018; EBA 2017). It has been emphasised that FinTech's rapid evolution may modify the risk profiles to which intermediaries and the financial markets are exposed and contribute to generating new, or amplifying existing, risks (EBA 2018c). Despite this, divergent opinions have emerged internationally on the need to regulate the FinTech phenomenon (BIS-FSB 2017).

This has led to slow decision-making on the action to be taken (Enria 2018) and brought a "wait-and-see" approach to the fore for some time (Arner et al. 2016; OICV-IOSCO 2017). This attitude by the regulators is called for when new and powerful technological innovations emerge because the authorities need to observe the new phenomenon before drawing up new rules, where extending the existing rules is not possible and/or advisable. Furthermore, the regulators must equip themselves with specific expertise as regards technological innovations in order to gain a clearer understanding of the scope and possible consequences of the innovations put forward by the new operators and the new business model used.[1]

It should be underlined that this wait-and-see approach as regards FinTech is also the outcome of a belief that the benefits expected from market digitalisation will outweigh the risks (BIS-FSB 2017; Enria 2018; FSB 2017). A premature legal intervention was held to be inopportune for two reasons. On one hand, regulation might reduce the financial sector's competitive, innovative and development potential, blocking the implementation of a series of advantages in terms of greater availability of innovative products, a multiplicity of channels, cost reductions and more efficient services for clients (BIS-FSB 2017). On the other hand, the risks generated by FinTech, including lower loan standards, the pro-cyclical impact and the emergence of aggressive pricing policies are not considered sufficiently serious to generate systemic risks, also in consideration of the limited scope of the phenomenon (FSB 2017).

Over time, the debate on the advisability of regulating FinTech came up against growth in FinTech and BigTech business volumes as well as concrete cases of regulatory arbitrage and limited transparency phenomena by some operators which have not infrequently resulted in episodes of crisis and fraud.[2] Thus a belief in the advisability of regulatory norms to safeguard stability and the correct functioning of the financial markets has grown (Bofondi and Gobbi 2017; Vives 2017). An awareness of the importance of coordinated international legal regulation of FinTech has also grown (Enria 2018; IMF 2018).

Light has been thrown on the fact that the survival of certain activity segments not subject to regulation and the co-existence of differentiated frameworks may lead to an increase in market risk to the detriment of the correct functioning of the financial systems, level playing field conditions and a potential lack of respect for client and investor safeguards (ESMA 2017a; IMF 2018). Furthermore, with specific reference to BigTech, it has been highlighted that, in the event that the financial services supplied are not subject to prudential regulations, risk management by these firms may be less well-developed and effective than regulated financial interme-diaries and this may constitute a market risk (FSB 2019).

It should also be added that the regulatory authorities have no power to sanction or to carry out checks on subjects not encompassed by their regulatory jurisdiction as defined by the law from time to time. The European Banking Authority highlighted this "legal vacuum" some time ago and came down in favour of the advisability of drawing up uniform European laws, especially for crowdfunding operators in consideration of the risks generated by their activities and to avoid regulatory arbitrage (directed at the European Commission, European Parliament and the European Union Council) (EBA 2015).

It is now commonly believed internationally that the objective of a new legal framework regarding financial innovation should be to reduce regu-latory arbitrage and provide a response proportional to risk (IMF 2018), taking into account the benefits of greater market competitivity and greater financial inclusion and channel diversification with the need to safeguards savers and investors (BIS-FSB 2017; IMF 2018).

5.2   European Action

European debates on the FinTech regulatory theme have, over time, high-lighted the risks and opportunities involved in financial market innovation and digitalisation. Debates around FinTech legal issues have taken place both at individual nation level and at the European level (European Commission 2017, 2018a) and led to the publication of an Action Plan regarding FinTech in 2018 (European Commission 2018a). The purpose of the European Commission's Action Plan was to foster a competitive and innovative financial market in three ways:

- encouraging the adoption of innovative business models;
- improving cybersecurity and IT management system resilience;
- supporting new technology adoption.

As regards the first aspect, the Commission drew up a series of legal interventions designed to establish across the board laws relating to access to markets by FinTech with uniform licensing standards, for example. The Commission drew up a regulatory proposal for crowdfunding (which we will look at in more detail in Sect. 5.2.2) and incentivised dialogue between the various operators involved in the digitalisation of the financial markets. From this perspective the Commission believes that creating "innovation facilitators" (or innovation hubs) and "regulatory sandboxes" is an effective way of encouraging knowledge and expertise exchanges between FinTech and incumbent firms and regulators (European Commission 2018a).

Effectively innovation facilitators and regulatory sandboxes have already been implemented in various regions. Australia, Japan, Hong Kong and Singapore are some of the states to have set up innovation hubs and regulatory sandboxes (BIS-BCBS 2018), testifying to the growing attention being paid to FinTech by the international regulatory authorities.

As far as Europe is concerned, innovation hubs have been set up in 21 EU member states and three Eastern European countries in different ways and involving diverse commitments by the regulatory authorities (ESAs 2018a), but with a shared overall objective of facilitating exchanges between FinTech and incumbent firms and the regulators.

There are fewer sandboxes, on the other hand, with five already active (Denmark, Lithuania, the Netherlands, Poland and the UK) and one which will begin work in 2019 (Norway) (ESAs 2018a). The purpose of the regulatory sandbox idea is to enable operators to test especially innovative business models, processes or products in a specific environment in order to evaluate their validity, sustainability and riskiness. This testing process takes place in accordance with regulatory provisions according to methods agreed with the regulatory authorities and is subject to ongoing monitoring by the latter (ESAs 2018a). Taking part in regulatory sandboxes does not involve exemptions or lightening of the burden of legal and regulatory obligations, where FinTech firms carry out limited or regulated activities on financial markets.

The solutions implemented with reference to the sandboxes are highly variegated in terms of the interaction between those involved, participation methods and specific objectives. In general, the sandboxes aim to raise awareness of the regulatory requisites by FinTech firms, increase the supervisory authorities' technological innovation know-how and foster innovation in the widest sense (ESAs 2018a).

A recent example is provided by the FinTech start-up firm 20|30, authorised by the Financial Conduct Authority (FCA) within its sandbox. The firm experimented in April 2019 the first Security Token Offering in a regulated stock market, thanks to the partnership with the London Stock Exchange (LSE). The same 20|30 will provide the platform for the tokenisation of the future issues admitted to trading.[3] The issue and the subsequent trading of a security token on the LSE constitutes a first institutional step towards the digital evolution of stock markets, thanks to the digitalisation of securities that allows eliminating most of the back-office operations linked to securities and allowing the securitisation of a wider array of assets.[4]

The sandbox theme was cited in a recent intervention by the vice president of the European Commission (Dombrovskis 2019), who argued for the importance of regulatory sandboxes and innovation hubs. He also announced the launching of the European Network of Innovation Facilitators on 2 April 2019 to facilitate co-ordination between the national authorities and allow firms taking part in the programme to achieve European scope more easily.

In addition to these initiatives, a series of legal and regulatory actions is emerging, in the European context, which is beginning to outline a regulatory framework for FinTech activities which we will examine in subsequent sections.[5]

5.2.1 Banking Activities

The FinTech phenomenon has led to the birth and development of digital banks and FinTech credit institutions. Whatever the technological or innovation level of the business, banking, as a regulated activity, requires a licence issued by the relevant authorities. In Europe this is the national authorities and the European Central Bank (ECB). In the light of an increase in banking licences granted to FinTech firms and the, to some extent, divergent attitude by some national authorities in relation to the procedure involved in checking and issuing banking licences, the ECB considers it important to intervene with guidelines. In particular, it issued banking licences to FinTech credit institution guidelines in 2018 (ECB 2018a, b) and in January 2019 published a comprehensive guide to the issuing of licences for both FinTech firms and traditional credit institutions (ECB 2019).

In a March 2018 document, the FinTech banks were defined by the ECB as banks with "*a business model in which the production and delivery of banking products and services are based on technology-enabled innovation*" (ECB 2018b). The FinTech bank guidelines clarify that providing banking services via platforms, with a lean organisational structure and via the use of technologically advanced tools does not exempt those engaging in it from the regulations applying to traditional banking institutions. The central bank considers that FinTech firms can be exposed to risks which are difficult to evaluate (including cyber risks) precisely because of the peculiarities of the service offered and the pronounced use of technologies. For this reason, it is possible that the ECB may require additional organisational, asset or governance requisites in the authorisation phase (ECB 2018a, b, c). In particular, the ECB guidelines highlight the need for asset and governance compliance and careful internal controls for FinTech firms wanting to expand their operations into banking. FinTech firms applying for licences to work in banking will thus have to guarantee compliance with the regulations and the governance skills and sustainability of their business models.

5.2.2   Marketplace Activities: Peer-to-Peer Lending and Equity Crowdfunding

As far as FinTech credit companies are concerned, in 2017 the European Banking Authority underlined that these frequently work outside the legal framework. Globally a recent update supplied by the Bank for International Settlements (Claessens et al. 2018) on the current FinTech credit regulation status quo has confirmed a variety of approaches. However, the direction taken by policy developments involves paying greater attention to regulating the sector. For example, Brazil and Mexico introduced specific lending via platform laws in early 2018, whilst Spain, the UK and Switzerland introduced minimum capital requirements for platforms from 2019 onwards (Claessens et al. 2018).

On a European level, one of the first countries to intervene on peer-to-peer lending was Italy. Banca d'Italia issued a regulation for the collection of savings by subjects different from banks ("Disposizioni in materia di raccolta del risparmio da parte dei soggetti diversi dalle banche"), in force since 2017 (Banca d'Italia 2016), which clarified the constraints within which peer-to-peer lending must take place if it is to avoid falling into the credit authorisation sphere. Platforms must comply with bans on collecting sight deposits and allow contracts based on personalised negotiations: borrowers and lenders should have the power to intervene on contract's clauses whilst platforms should limit themselves to supporting activities. In the event that this does not occur, such as when platforms have a stake in loans (including a share of them), they are acting as credit intermediaries and must have licences (e.g. in consumer credit and factoring).

Also with reference to equity crowdfunding, one of the first countries in the world to require specific regulations was Italy (OICV-IOSCO 2017). In fact, as early as 2013, the national authority on the markets (Consob) published regulations applicable to online portal management and capital collection provision, requiring entry criteria for equity crowdfunding operators and their functioning methods.[6] Since 2013, then, firms operating in equity crowdfunding in Italy have had to be licensed by Consob and registered. Over time other countries have also established functioning rules for equity crowdfunding platforms and drawn up specific laws to protect savers including: investment limits for retail investors; investor right to withdraw within a specified period from the investment; a ban on providing investment advice on a firm's own site and mandatory conduct (OICV-IOSCO 2017).

The risks inherent in this fragmentation in regulatory approaches on the marketplace on a Europe wide level have prompted the European authorities to intervene with their own specific policy. A first version was published in March 2018, by the European Commission. The objective of this intervention was to delineate a clearer regulatory framework in accordance with the wishes of the International Monetary Fund (IMF 2018) which, in the context of the Bali FinTech Agenda, highlighted the need to adapt the regulatory framework and supervisory practices to the advent of FinTech in order to foster an ordered market development and ensure stability, monitoring the risks and promoting consumer trust.

The European choice would thus appear to be to draw up specific crowdfunding regulations which do not apply the same rules applying to regulated intermediaries and financial markets.[7]

This regulation proposal requires lending and equity crowdfunding platforms to adopt governance procedures guaranteeing transparency, controls over investors' financial know-how and their ability to sustain any losses.

The original version of the European regulations involved issuing authorisations for crowdfunding platforms on condition that these work in a standardised legal environment and, certainly, with the chance to work in conditions of reciprocal recognition in all member states (European Commission 2018b). Initial proposals to subject these to the European Securities and Markets Authority (ESMA) supervision were then left out of the subsequent version which took on board certain amendments (ECON 2018b), drawing on a series of other aspects summarised in Table 5.1. In general, the amended version retained the idea of setting up a regulatory framework, requiring minimum capital sums for platforms and establishing maximum thresholds for investments (above all to protect retail investors). The Initial Coin Offerings (ICOs) are also mentioned and the relative risks clarified.

5.2.3   *Financial Advice and Investment Services*

The digitalisation of the financial markets has allowed for the development of advisory and digitalised asset management services. Despite provision via technologically avant-garde tools (including robo advice) these activities are subject to provisions applying to traditional investment financial advice and services (in particular, for Europe, MiFID II and the Alternative Investment Fund Managers Directive (or AIFMD)). Proposals involving investing in specific financial tools formulated for clients are explicitly cited in the regulations as the exclusive preserve of regulated entities. The regulatory challenge in this context is thus not a matter of understanding whether the regulations should apply to FinTechs interfacing as consultants: these carry out regulated activities and must thus necessarily be authorised as financial intermediaries or, if they give independent financial advice, be officially registered as independent consultants (AA.VV. 2019).

The truly critical issue in this sphere is the fact that not all FinTechs operating in the investment area overtly offer clients financial advice and investment services (EBA 2018c). Certain FinTech firms present potential theoretical portfolios, including via robo advice or algorithms, which clients can construct on the basis of their own characteristics (i.e. the data which have fed the algorithm). Others supply technological type tools

Table 5.1 European regulatory proposal on marketplaces: proposed amendments

Provisions	Note
Regulatory regime, saver safeguards and supervisory activities	
Offer threshold	Increase in thresholds to 8 million euros for platforms from the 1 million required in the first draft. The value required in the first draft cited the threshold value for the publication of prospectuses in accordance with European regulation. The new statement, on the other hand, takes account of the fact that certain member states currently have higher thresholds. The Commission argued that retaining a lower threshold for crowdfunding than for prospectus limits (higher) could make crowdfunding less attractive
Authorisations for platform and institution operators for supervisory regimes by the authorities	In contrast to the first draft, the amendments would seem to accord primary responsibility in this sphere to national authorities, which act in accordance with a common supervisory framework and report to ESMA. The proposal also foresees extending the opportunity to work in Europe by third-party crowdfunding platforms demonstrating compliance with the standard required for European platforms
Proportionality according to business model	Differentiated regimes for the most straightforward platforms (which facilitate investor and project proposer matching) and for the more advanced platforms
Proposed maximum investment thresholds for retail clients	At present no single value has been established but annual and single investment limits have been set
Platform obligations	
Minimum capital	The proposal cites a minimum capital or an insurance contract to cover any damage potentially deriving from failure to fulfil legal requirements
Project default rate	Default rate disclosure for projects funded via the platform.
Due diligence and project evaluation	Crowdfunding platforms will have to check the following aspects: • the absence of convictions for failure to comply with commercial, bankruptcy, financial services, anti-money laundering, fraud and professional responsibility laws; • the headquarters of the firm promoting the project on the platform must not be on a list of non-co-operating countries, high-risk countries or those not complying with EU or international transparency and information exchange standards
Disclosure level	Where possible, firms proposing projects must publish profitability, liquidity and efficiency statements. Platforms must check the truthfulness of the data and publish it in comparable format
ICOs	Planned further standards and norms for operations and platforms involving ICOs as well as defining consumer safeguard tools. Once again on the ICO theme, certain amendments supply a formal definition of the tools and make risks explicit: market, fraud and cybersecurity risks

Source: The authors' elaboration of European Commission (2018b) and ECON (2018a, b) data (platforms or apps) which enable investors to replicate the strategies of other traders enrolled on the same platform (so-called copy trading). In such cases whilst it is true that such Fintech firms do not directly supply advice they can certainly orientate users' investments decisions (ESAs 2016) whilst not being subject to the regulations and consequently without having to comply with provisions generally set up to protect investors, including dispositions on suitability, transparency, accuracy and conflict of interest disclosure.

As regards robo advisor activities—considered especially innovative— the European authorities have repeatedly emphasised the need for such products and services to comply with legal standards in all phases of product creation and service provision from product governance to marketing and distribution via the various channels (both telematic and physical) and post-sales safeguards (above all as regards complaints management) (ESMA 2017b, 2018).

The European authorities have frequently intervened on this theme, highlighting the potential benefits of such solutions and their related risks, contributing to the debate on the advisability of drawing up specific laws (ESAs 2015, 2016; EBA 2018c). The authorities have also highlighted the risks potentially arising from automised advisory services linked to the following factors: limited transparency and the inadequacy of the information supplied to investors as a basis for their decisions; errors in the functioning of the tools due to algorithm bias; the manipulation of these and cyberattacks; legal risks relating to limited asset allocation process transparency and, as a result of the potential lack of explicit agreements between the parties to the service partnership (e.g. FinTech and the banks), risks of market orientation in the direction of specific financial tools where different investors use robo advisor services to replace human consultants (ESAs 2016, 2018c). Recently, the ESAs (2018c) have highlighted that robo advisor services are currently primarily being offered by authorised financial intermediaries, although sometimes in partnership with FinTech firms specialising in robo advice (including via the white labelling mechanism). In consideration of this and the fact that the growth registered is slow and the risks feared by the authorities have not arisen, the ESAs argue that specific regulations are not currently required (ESAs 2018c). However, the attention of the authorities remains high and monitoring by regulators and supervisors into market development and, in particular, potential risk to investors has continued (ESMA 2018; EBA 2018c).

5.2.4   Payments

The payment area was the first area of FinTech development and it is still one of its most active, in terms both of operator numbers and volumes. As far as current laws and regulations are concerned, FinTech and BigTech had to apply for licences right from the start as legal tender transfers are the exclusive preserve of financial intermediaries. In the European context the BigTechs have formed subsidiaries with head offices in European countries and FinTech firms with head offices in one EU country can operate across the European Union on the strength of European "passports" acquired when they obtain a licence in a member state.

In the payment area entities, authorised as payment institutions or electronic money institutions (ELMIs) and those relying on authorised third parties (payment institutions or ELMIs) both operate. In this area of activity the coming into force of the new European Payment Services Directive (or PSD2) is a significant break with the past, with considerable fallout for the banking industry as it opens the way to open banking (EBA 2018b). Furthermore, this directive allows third-party providers (TPPs) access to data relating to banking clients' current accounts on condition that current account holders give their consent. This applies solely to TPPs subject to supervisor controls, however (EBA 2018b; Schena et al. 2018; Scopsi 2018). As we saw briefly in Sect. 2.2.3, this legal intervention, together with regulations on free cross-border circulation of data and information processing security (General Data Protection Regulation), will have a significant influence on competitive dynamics in financial markets in terms of access to information used to supply personalised services.

The new laws on data processing and payments may, however, constitute an opportunity for the banks too, as they may access their client information held by other FinTech or BigTech firms, on permission from clients. In this way, incumbent firms may be able to exploit personal data and big data to design and propose more personalised products and services rapidly and efficiently. This may bring with it certain advantages for clients themselves.

5.2.5   Crypto Currencies

There is still a very uneven regulatory playing field internationally as far as crypto currencies are concerned, principally as a result of the fact that, at the moment, macro-economic problems, impacts for the central banks and risks of displacement of legal tender are not considered to be on the horizon (Lastra and Allen 2018; Claeys et al. 2018). This does not, however, rule out the risks inherent in virtual currencies. In fact, the issue of potential problems relating to monetary policy transmission mechanisms remains topical,[8] as do the difficulties which can derive from the decision to regulate only potentially risky ex-post phenomena.[9]

The central Japanese bank adopted a favourable approach to crypto currencies and Bitcoin was accorded legal tender status there in 2017, in a regulated market.[10] In a comparable way, the Swiss Financial Market Supervisory Authority (FINMA) authorised banking product and service provision in digital currency terms and regulated Initial Coin Offerings (FINMA 2018). In China, a free use of virtual currencies was allowed up to 2017, although these were not accorded legal tender status. Subsequently, the government and the central bank (People's Bank of China—PBC) banned virtual currencies, considering their circulation as a market currency to be unacceptable because of their lack of legal value (PBC 2017). The authorities also banned Initial Coin Offerings (PBC 2017), closed local markets in which virtual currencies were used and applied sanctions to these with the objective of blocking the crypto currencies market which had continued to develop in the face of legal restrictions via foreign sites and offshore platforms (Reuters 2018).

The European Union's approach was, by contrast, more cautious and whilst such currencies were not made illegal, virtual currencies have been cited in various circumstances as an especially risky asset (ECB 2012; EBA 2014; ESAs 2018b; European Parliament 2016). In particular, the authorities have called for client caution in consideration of risks linked not only to the volatility and limited liquidity of these assets but also the fact that crypto currencies platforms are not currently subject to supervisory controls nor anti-money laundering laws and can thus become illegal money, tax evasion and fraud against client channels (ESAs 2018b; Underwood 2018). It should also be added that virtual currencies were the subject of European Council and Parliament directive 2018/843, in the context of the wider issue of preventing the financial system from being used for money laundering or terrorism funding purposes. The directive's provisions comprise an obligation for the European Union's member states to introduce digital money status into their legal frameworks by January 2020.

Recent intervention by EBA (2019), at the behest of the European Commission, has also underlined the fact that this area is still outside the regulatory framework. At the same time, the EBA has emphasised that certain member states are considering legislating crypto asset platforms, virtual currencies wallets and crypto currencies activities (e.g. investment or security tokens) of their own accord and some have already implemented these. For EBA, these non-standardised provisions risk creating a misalignment in European legal frameworks on crypto asset providers, generating areas of potential legal arbitrage. Furthermore, the authorities consider that, whilst crypto currencies development in Europe is still limited, the risks linked to their use are significant. For this reason, a standard approach to the matter is desirable to protect consumers, safeguard the resilience and integrity of the markets and guarantee a level playing field (EBA 2019).

Lastly, it should be highlighted that financial instruments based on crypto currencies or in which these are implicit are subject to financial instrument laws as ESMA (2017c) and the British Financial Conduct Authority make clear (FCA 2017a, b, c). In line with this approach the American market authorities (Security and Exchange Commission) have decided that Initial Coin Offerings are covered by their remit and have intervened repeatedly to block fraudulent ICOs or fine non-transparent operators.[11]

NOTES

1. The route taken by the New York Federal Reserve involved setting up a Fintech Advisory Group made up of exponents of the finance industry and technology firms for the purpose of improving the authority's innovation-related know-how and fostering debate with operators (New York Fed 2019).
2. For an analysis of certain cases of crisis, see BIS/FSB (2017) and, in particular, crisis experiences by FinTech credit operators in the USA, China and Sweden, all generated by fraud. For an analysis of the current FinTech credit uneven legal playing field, see Claessens et al. (2018).
3. See https://www.telegraph.co.uk/technology/2019/04/15/london-stock-exchange-accepts-first-listing-blockchain-token/.
4. The characteristics of security tokens and the underlying smart contracts make a series of operation run by the various financial intermediaries involved in the traditional securities trading superfluous.
5. For further details, see Barbagallo (2018), Carstens (2018), and EBA (2017, 2018a, b).
6. The regulations issued by Consob in 2013 were amended in 2016 and 2017 (Consob 2017).

7. The 2017/1129 EU regulation relating to the statement to be published for public prospectus and admission to securities bargaining in a regulated market sets out an exemption from the obligation to issue for sums below a defined minimum threshold. The European Commission (2018b) proposed a maximum threshold of 8 million euros, below which small and medium-sized enterprises accessing a crowdfunding platform must not be considered issuers of public shares for legal purposes.

8. The existence of alternative payment systems to legal tender which do not pass through regulated financial intermediaries can reduce the efficacy of the monetary transmission strategies implemented by the central banks (European Parliament 2016) in the event that monetary resources start to flow out of banks accounts into virtual wallets or other alternative solutions.

9. Once again the Chinese experience offers some interesting insights. China was one of the main global crypto currencies markets, on the strength of the great freedom accorded platforms to set up and develop activities. In 2017, the Chinese government decided to ban both initial coin offerings (ICOs), and the circulation and use of virtual currencies whose legal value is not recognised (PBC 2017). Applying this ruling proved difficult because virtual money exchanges continued to take place in China in the face of the ban, via the use of foreign sites and offshore platforms.

10. As a result of crypto currencies regulations and the dissemination of the platform, the Japanese market authorities acted against two platforms in 2018, blocking their operations in the aftermath of a serious cyberattack which led to huge investor losses and required significant improvements in anti-money laundering policy terms from a further eight platforms (Financial Times 2018).

11. See the ICO Updates section on https://www.sec.gov/ICO.

References

AA.VV. (2019, January). *La digitalizzazione della consulenza in materia di investimenti finanziari [Digitalisation in financial advice for financial investments].* Quaderno FinTech, n. 3.

Arner, D. W., Barberis, J., & Buckley, R. P. (2016). The evolution of FinTech: New post-crisis paradigm. *Georgetown Journal of International Law, 47*(4), 1271–1320.

Banca d'Italia. (2016, November 8). *Provvedimento recante disposizioni per la raccolta del risparmio dei soggetti diversi dalle banche [Provisions for the collection of savings from parties other than banks].*

Barbagallo, C. (2018, July 23). *Fintech and the future of financial services.* Speech by the Director General for Financial Supervision and Regulation, Bank of Italy at the International Summer School Banking & Capital Markets Law, Milan.

BIS-BCBS. (2018, February). *Sound practices. Implications of fintech developments for banks and bank supervisors.* Basel Committee on Banking Supervision—BIS. Retrieved March 27, 2019, from https://www.bis.org/bcbs/publ/d431.pdf.

BIS-FSB. (2017, May 22). *FinTech credit: Market structure, business models and financial stability implications.* Report prepared by a Working Group established by the Committee on the Global Financial System (CGFS—Bank of International Settlement) and the Financial Stability Board.

Bofondi, M., & Gobbi, G. (2017). The big promise of Fintech. *European Economy,* 2, 107–119.

Carstens, A. (2018, December 4). *Big tech in finance and new challenges for public policy.* Keynote address by the General Manager, Bank for International Settlements, FT Banking Summit, London.

Claessens, S., Frost, J., Turner, G., & Zhu, F. (2018, September). Fintech credit markets around the world: Size, drivers and policy issues. *BIS Quarterly Review.*

Claeys, G., Demertzis, M., & Efstathiou, K. (2018). *Cryptocurrencies and monetary policy.* Monetary Dialogue July 2018—European Parliament; this study was provided by Policy Department A at the request of the European Parliament's Committee on Economic and Monetary Affairs. Retrieved March 27, 2019, from http://www.europarl.europa.eu/committees/en/econ/monetary-dialogue.html.

Consob. (2017). *Regolamento sulla raccolta di capitali di rischio tramite portali on-line—Adottato con delibera n. 18592 del 26 giugno 2013 e Aggiornato con le modifiche apportate dalla delibera n. 20204 del 29 novembre 2017 [Regulation on the collection of risk capital through online portals—Adopted with resolution no. 18592 of June 26, 2013 and updated with the changes made by resolution no. 20204 of 29 November 2017].*

Dombrovskis, D. (2019, February 26). Speech by the vice-president of European Commission at the Afore Consulting—3rd Annual Fintech Conference, Brussels.

EBA. (2014, July 4). *Opinion on "virtual currencies".* EBA/Op/2014/08.

EBA. (2015, February 26). *Opinion of the European banking authority on lending-based crowdfunding.* EBA/Op/2015/03.

EBA. (2017, August 4). *Discussion paper on the EBA's approach to financial technology (FinTech).* EBA/DP/2017/02.

EBA. (2018a, March 15). *The EBA's fintech roadmap, conclusions from the consultation on the Eba's approach to financial technology (Fintech).*

EBA. (2018b, July 3). *EBA report on the impact of Fintech on incumbent credit institutions' business models.*

EBA. (2018c, July 3). *EBA report on the prudential risks and opportunities arising for institutions from Fintech.*

EBA. (2019, January 9). *Report with advice for the European Commission on crypto-assets.* EBA Report.

ECB. (2012, October). *Virtual currency schemes.*

ECB. (2018a, March). *Guide to assessments of licence applications. Licence applications in general.*

ECB. (2018b, March). *Guide to assessments of fintech credit institution licence applications.*

ECB. (2018c, June). *Survey on the access to finance of enterprises in the euro area.*

ECB. (2019, January). *Guide to assessments of licence applications, licence applications in general.*

ECON. (2018a). *Draft report, Ashley Fox, European Crowdfunding Service Providers (ECSP) for business proposal for a regulation.* (COM(2018)0113—C8-0103/2018—2018/0048(COD)).

ECON. (2018b). *Draft report, Caroline Nagtegaal (PE625.579v01-00), markets in financial instruments, proposal for a directive.* (COM(2018)0099—C8-0102/2018—2018/0047(COD)).

Enria, A. (2018, March 9). *Designing a regulatory and supervisory roadmap for FinTech.* Speech by the Chairperson of the European Banking Authority (EBA), Copenhagen Business School.

ESAs. (2015, dicembre 5). *JC discussion paper (DP) on automation in financial advice.* JC 2015 080.

ESAs. (2016). *Report on automation in financial advice.* Retrieved March 27, 2019, from https://esas-joint-committee.europa.eu/Publications/Reports/EBA%20BS%202016%20422%20(JC%20SC%20CPFI%20Final%20Report%20on%20automated%20advice%20tools).pdf.

ESAs. (2018a). *FinTech: Regulatory sandboxes and innovation hubs.* JC 2018 74. Retrieved March 27, 2019, from https://eba.europa.eu/documents/10180/2545547/JC+2018+74+Joint+Report+on+Regulatory+Sandboxes+and+Innovation+Hubs.pdf.

ESAs. (2018b). *Warning—ESMA, EBA and EIOPA warn consumers on the risks of virtual currencies.* Retrieved March 27, 2019, from https://www.esma.europa.eu/press-news/esma-news/esas-warn-consumers-risks-in-buying-virtual-currencies.

ESAs. (2018c, September 5). *Joint Committee report on the results of the monitoring exercise on 'automation in financial advice'.* JC 2018-29.

ESMA. (2017a, June 7). *ESMA response to the commission consultation paper on Fintech: A more competitive and innovative financial sector.* ESMA50-158-457.

ESMA. (2017b). *MiFID II e protezione degli investitori—consulenza e valutazione di adeguatezza [MiFID II and investors protection—Financial advice and ade-*

quacy evaluation]. Speech by Gnoni S., Investor Protection and Intermediaries—ESMA.

ESMA. (2017c, December 15). *Statement on preparatory work of the European securities and markets authority in relation to CFDs and binary options offered to retail clients.* ESMA71-99-910.

ESMA. (2018). *Guidelines on MiFID II product governance requirements.* ESMA35-43-620.

European Commission. (2017, March 23). *Consultation document—FinTech: A more competitive and innovative financial sector.*

European Commission. (2018a). *FinTech action plan: For a more competitive and innovative European financial sector.* COM(2018)109/F1.

European Commission. (2018b, March 8). *Proposal for a regulation of the European Parliament and of the Council on European Crowdfunding Service Providers (ECSP) for business.* COM(2018) 113 final, 2018/0048 (COD), Brussels.

European Parliament. (2016). *Resolution of 26 May 2016 on virtual currencies (2016/2007(INI)).* P8-TA(2016)0228.

FCA. (2017a, April). *Discussion paper on distributed ledger technology (DP17/3).* https://www.fca.org.uk/publication/discussion/dp17-03.pdf.

FCA. (2017b, September 12). *Consumer warning about the risks of initial coin offerings ('ICOs'), statements.* Retrieved March 27, 2019, from https://www.fca.org.uk/news/statements/initial-coin-offerings.

FCA. (2017c, November 14). *Consumer warning about the risks of investing in cryptocurrency CFDs.* Retrieved March 27, 2019, from https://www.fca.org.uk/news/news-stories/consumer-warning-about-risks-investing-cryptocurrency-cfds.

Financial Times. (2018, March 8). *Japan suspends trade on 2 cryptocurrency exchanges.* Retrieved March 27, 2019, from https://www.ft.com/content/24f818e8-2276-11e8-9a70-08f715791301.

FINMA. (2018, February 16). *Guidelines for enquiries regarding the regulatory framework for initial coin offerings (ICOs).*

FSB. (2017, June 27). *Financial stability implications from FinTech, supervisory and regulatory issues that merit authorities' attention.*

FSB. (2019, February 14). *FinTech and market structure in financial services: Market developments and potential financial stability implications.*

IMF. (2018, October). *The Bali Fintech Agenda.* IMF policy paper. Retrieved March 27, 2019, from http://www.imf.org/external/pp/ppindex.aspx.

Lastra, R. M., & Allen, J. G. (2018). *Virtual currencies in the Eurosystem: Challenges ahead.* Monetary Dialogue July 2018—European Parliament; this study was provided by Policy Department A at the request of the European Parliament's Committee on Economic and Monetary Affairs. Retrieved March 27, 2019, from http://www.europarl.europa.eu/committees/en/econ/monetary-dialogue.html.

New York Fed. (2019, March 22). New York Fed launches Fintech advisory group. *Press Release.* Retrieved March 27, 2019, from https://www.newyorkfed.org/newsevents/news/aboutthefed/2019/20190322.

OICV-IOSCO. (2017, February). *IOSCO research report on financial technologies (Fintech).*

PBC. (2017). *Public notice of the PBC, CAC, MIIT, SAIC, CBRC, CSRC and CIRC on preventing risks of fundraising through coin offering.* Retrieved March 27, 2019, from http://www.pbc.gov.cn/english/130721/3377816/index. html?__hstc=172477884.47f4fea8ab884286c11d72f5acbde d2a.1512086400087.1512086400088.1512086400089.1&__hssc=1724778 84.1.1512086400090&__hsfp=528229161.

Reuters. (2018, June 1). *China steps up regulation of fast-growing money market funds.* Retrieved January 15, 2018, from https://www.reuters.com/article/us-china-bitcoin/pboc-official-says-chinas-centralized-virtual-currency-trade-needs-to-end-source-idUSKBN1F50FZ.

Schena, C., Tanda, A., Arlotta, C., & Potenza, G. (2018, March). *The development of FinTech. Opportunities and risks for the financial industry in the digital era.* Consob—FinTech papers, no. 1. Retrieved March 28, 2019, from http://www.consob.it/web/area-pubblica/ft1.

Scopsi, M. (2018). *The expansion of big data companies in the financial services industry, and EU regulation.* IAI papers 19/06.

Underwood, B. D. (2018, September 18). *Virtual markets integrity initiative.* Office of the New York State Attorney General.

Vives, X. (2017). The impact of Fintech on banking. *European Economy, 2,* 97–105.

Zetzsche, D. A., Buckley, R. P., Arner, D. W., & Barberis, J. N. (2017). *From FinTech to TechFin: The regulatory challenges of data-driven finance.* EBI working paper series, no. 6.

CHAPTER 6

An Attempt at Synthesis: Financial Market Digitalisation Scenarios, Opportunities and Challenges

Abstract The FinTech revolution has changed the financial markets which are now facing a point of no return. New products, services and processes are being offered by new entrants, be they FinTech, BigTech or digital native financial intermediaries. A competitive power that mainly derives from the new business models adopted for the provision of financial services is forcing incumbent banks to rethink their approach to the market and to customers. BigTech and FinTech represent worrying competitors, but also an opportunity for partnerships, especially for smaller banks. The future development of banking business models will also be shaped by the regulatory steps that will be taken by the authorities. These should aim to level the playing field to ensure financial stability and consumer protection.

Keywords FinTech • BigTech • Information • Banking business model • Digitalisation

6.1 The FinTech Revolution and the Pivotal Role of Information

This work has highlighted the multiplicity of strategic approaches and business models adopted by the various types of new operators working in the field of financial intermediation characteristic of the banks (e.g. FinTech, BigTech and challenger banks), comparing these with incum-

© The Author(s) 2019   101
A. Tanda, C.-M. Schena, *FinTech, BigTech and Banks*, Palgrave
Macmillan Studies in Banking and Financial Institutions,
https://doi.org/10.1007/978-3-030-22426-4_6

bent firms of various sizes and operational vocations. The change currently underway is in some ways radical and the result of applying technology to the search for market spaces not sufficiently covered by the traditional banks and retail clients in particular.

A first element which emerges clearly is that, in a data-driven-type economy, the quality of the information underlying financial service provision to clients and the way it is processed is significant. Applying an artificial intelligence system to big data elaboration (BDAI) offers the potential to significantly improve the rapidity, cost and efficacy of data analysis in support of clients' financial decisions. At the same time, the lack of transparency, in the ways the artificial intelligence algorithms used to assign risk categories by FinTech are worked out, raises important question marks over the quality and accuracy of these algorithms and, consequently, on their effective usefulness from the standpoint of the clients to whom these financial services are offered. The theme is even more delicate in consideration, on one hand, of the proliferation of direct financial circuits within which the financial risks generally fall on the clients and not on the FinTech companies and, on the other, the approach of the BigTech firms which store big data and seek to act as exclusive interlocutors for all types of client needs.[1]

As BaFin has highlighted (2018) "consumer data sovereignty enables trust in BDAI innovations", on condition that it is possible "to gain and maintain the trust of consumers by ensuring that their data is used as desired and in accordance with the law. Besides the technical approaches that allow for anonymised analyses, consumer data sovereignty could represent another approach. Consumers can only make a sovereign decision if they are adequately informed about the potential reach and consequences of the use of their data, if they are given reliable options for controlling how their data is used, and if they have actual freedom of choice. Providers are responsible for ensuring that these requirements are fulfilled".

Clients' effective freedom and ability to choose is an especially important issue, both in the light of the financial expertise of the retail client segment which generally turns to the new financial operators and of the fact that these latter are not generally subject to codes of conduct designed to safeguard client interests. The risk is thus that the expected benefits of financial innovations are, in actual fact, rhetorical[2] and can lead to "information oligopolies" capable of channelling client choices in the financial context, too, without taking account of their real needs. Moreover, this theme—which is today generally traceable to BigTech in consideration of its competitive advantage in terms of the availability of especially advanced technology—could become even more problematic.

In the course of his hearing at the American Senate in the context of the Hearings on FinTech, Omarova emphasised that, in her view, the vast deregulation strategy via incentives to the banks to form partnerships with data mining firms may potentially generate considerable risks: setting aside the principle of separation between banking and commerce—a fundamental one in American banking law—would allow the banks and retail businesses to build ever more intense relationships and could generate the creation of excessive concentrations of financial and market power, opening the door to "conglomerates that will control the flow of both money and information and effectively take control of our lives, not only as economic actors but also as citizens" (Omarova 2018).

6.2   The Legal and Regulatory Challenge

A second issue, closely bound up with the first, is, in our opinion, especially significant and relates to the legal framework within which these new market dynamics are developing. The current laws cannot encompass all FinTech's operational innovations and are also extremely unstandardised internationally. This leaves room for regulatory arbitrage and allows FinTech to escape all forms of regulation altogether, in many cases and in the operational areas analysed by us here.

To date, the prevailing opinion of the regulators and the supervisory authorities is that FinTech does not generate systemic risks for various spheres of financial activity. However, the experience of the Chinese market, cited in this work, highlights a series of aspects which provide food for thought: on one hand, the concrete possibility that FinTech can generate stability risks for the financial system and, on the other, the effects that the absence of investor protection can determine, not solely for individual clients but also on savings safeguards and the ability to effectively channel financial resources in support of economic development.

We have also underlined that financial digitalisation enables geographic boundaries to be overcome, making efforts to regulate individual nation states especially futile unless these form part of an organic supranational regulation framework. This latter objective is, for various reasons, difficult to achieve and in this context, the European Union has launched an attempt to update its legal framework also in accordance with the

European Commission's Action Plan (2018). We believe that this is important in ensuring consumer protection and, in the same way, increasing clients' trust in financial services providers and stimulating further development. The legal framework which has developed thus far is still limited to certain specific themed areas referred to in the course of this work and does not take on board the issue of homogeneous regulation by activity but still focuses on the type of operator offering financial services.

The creation of a level playing field to protect clients' interests and the stability of the financial system should be the principle underlying the authorities' efforts. It is in the light of the legal changes to be implemented to deal with the changes caused by digitalisation that the winning and sustainable financial operator business model will take shape.

6.3   THE NEW BUSINESS MODELS AND THE FUTURE ROLE OF INCUMBENT FIRMS

What has been outlined thus far explains how the current competitive dynamics between financial operators did not develop in the context of a level playing field and that the strategic choices made by the banks were influenced by criteria and constraints defined by the regulatory framework in which their activities take place. In fact, the banks involved in developing strategies in line with market and technological innovations have to identify business models which will turn out to generate long term value as well as being economically sustainable and legally compliant.[3]

In the course of this work, a powerful capacity for innovation has emerged amongst FinTech operators, based on financial unbundling and rebundling which enables them to make their financial services especially user-friendly and offer clients a suitably structured response to their financial needs. Via specific reference to BigTech, core business reinforcement strategies and marked financial activity diversification and development have emerged. In any event, being able to interact with a consolidated client base, use and elaborate the big data available to them and the dynamic nature of the technological and operational solutions which have emerged, as well as attention to client satisfaction, have enabled BigTech to achieve a hugely significant level of financial services development and operate on the market as effective competitors to the largest incumbent banks.

It should be underlined that BigTech, perhaps to an even greater extent than FinTech, has developed a series of partnerships with incumbent firms and not only where these were potentially functional to evading requests for banking licences and thus compliance with supervisory norms. In this work it has, in fact, emerged that the Chinese BigTech firms, which have also created banks and other financial firms within their groups with especially large operational volumes, have also continued to work with incumbent firms. This approach effectively enables BigTech firms to present "integrated platforms" on which clients can buy services from various providers and, at the same time, offer their own products and services including via other financial intermediaries and operators.

Our analysis of the new digital native banks has also provided food for thought. In the first place, it has emerged that the independent challenger banks, on a par with other FinTech operators, are adopting business models which are a long way away from the traditional banking models used by incumbents (both traditional and online). These can offer innovative products not to be found on traditional circuits and not operate simultaneously in traditional collection of savings and lending functions, testifying to their radically different conception of banking as compared to that foreseen by existing legislation. In the second place, it has enabled us to highlight the different roles that native digital banks can play within BigTech and incumbent groups. In the former, these act primarily as captive banks to increase service provision to the clients acquired by the BigTech parent company. In the latter, digital native banks can enable banking groups to segment their reference clients into the group's individual firms and offer financial services by means of technologically advanced solutions in shorter time frames than those required to upgrade the group's technological framework as a whole.

As regards the incumbent firms, we have analysed the main international players and the smaller banks separately. As far as the larger international banks examined are concerned, an awareness of the need to grasp the opportunities offered by technological evolutions and respond proactively to the challenges posed by the new market scenarios emerges. The main individual bank initiatives examined bring out the great investment made in digital development and the various approaches resorted to (in-house, share acquisition and partnerships) adopted by the banks. At the same time the diverse intensity of these initiatives within the individual banks is visible. Still today efforts have primarily targeted the digital transformation and updating of the distribution network rather than the productive front. This may reflect the difficulties encountered by complex group structures in effectively implementing the strategic and operational changes required by the new digitalisation context.

The competitive threat generated by all the new types of financial operations (FinTech, BigTech and native digital banks) would appear to be especially marked for the smaller banks for two reasons. First of all, because the new operators primarily offer their services to retail clients (individuals and small and medium-sized enterprises) to whom they ensure "digital proximity" which goes beyond the geographical confines in small-medium-sized bank field of action. In the second place, the smaller banks have more limited financial and human resources available to them for technological investments and their effective implementation. The examples shown indicate seeking out a partnership as an effective option.

It is not clear which future change scenario will come to the fore in the banking and financial sector from those identified in the various studies effectively summarised in a recent report by BIS-BCBS (2018). However, the overall results which have emerged from this study contribute to the next generation of banking business model debate, offering wide-ranging insights for policy takers and policy makers on the strengths and weaknesses of the various strategic approaches and the many business models adopted to date in the activities of the various types of banking operator. In particular, to date the extreme scenarios outlined by the Basel Committee, envisaging a future financial system in which incumbents will succeed in coming to the fore as single operators ("better bank") or, on the opposite extreme, a system in which clients will prefer to interface with FinTech and BigTech for all their financial needs ("disintermediated bank") (BIS-BCBS 2018) do not seem plausible. We have, in fact, seen that the demarcation line between banks, native digital banks (challenger banks) and FinTech will become progressively less clear as bank digitalisation moves forward.

At the same time, this analysis clearly highlights that the future scenarios may move in the direction of one or other extreme in accordance with the degree of FinTech pervasiveness which may grow further and rapidly in the current legal context and in accordance with the degree of efficacy of the incumbents' response strategies. What has emerged is that FinTech firms, and BigTech in particular, are moving rapidly in the direction of an integrated service platform model and this shortens the time frames available to the banks in which to develop strategic plans enabling them to play anything but a merely ancillary role ("relegated banking" or "distributed banking", according to the indications of the Basel Committee).

However, the response of the banks to the financial activity digitalisation challenge is still slow and, as yet, indecisive in productive terms. It is also clear that distribution channel digitalisation and setting up online banking and apps accessing financial services do not themselves ensure operational development and are no longer a competitive advantage but rather a pre-requisite in the context of changing client needs. The banks are thus facing a more complex challenge linked to the decision not to give up client relations, whilst being clear about the goal of developing services with higher added values in the context of the client segments they are targeting.

Notes

1. It is a theme which raises many delicate questions relating to data protection, privacy and appropriate use of information by big data "managers" including in relation to fully competitive profiles (European Commission 2017).
2. Omarova (2018) has highlighted that "*Today, the same rhetoric of financial innovation and consumer choice that brought us the financial crisis of 2008 returns to center stage in the policy debate over fintech (...) Once again, new technologies promise to make the system more efficient, resilient, and democratic; to expand consumer choices; and to give low-income Americans access to financial services*".
3. The issue of the sustainability of the business model (in the short and long term) constitutes a key issue in European vigilance which incorporated it as one of its Supervisory Review and Evaluation Process analysis components in 2016 (ECB 2018).

References

BaFin (Bundesanstalt für Finanzdienstleistungsaufsicht). (2018, July). *Big data meets artificial intelligence. Challenges and implications for the supervision and regulation of financial services.*

BIS-BCBS. (2018, February). *Sound practices. Implications of fintech developments for banks and bank supervisors.* Basel Committee on Banking Supervision—BIS. Retrieved March 27, 2019, from https://www.bis.org/bcbs/publ/d431.pdf.

ECB (European Central Bank). (2018, September). *SSM thematic review on profitability and business models.* Report on the outcome of the assessment.

European Commission. (2017). *Building a European data economy.* COM(2017) no. 9.

European Commission. (2018). *FinTech action plan: For a more competitive and innovative European financial sector.* COM(2018)109/F1.

Omarova, S. T. (2018, September 18). *New Tech V. New Deal: Fintech as a systemic phenomenon.* Written Testimony of Saule T. Omarova, Professor of Law Cornell University, Before the United States Senate—Committee on Banking, Housing, and Urban Affairs, Fintech: Examining Digitization, Data, and Technology.

Index[1]

---

[1] Note: Page numbers followed by 'n' refer to notes.

© The Author(s) 2019
A. Tanda, C.-M. Schena, *FinTech, BigTech and Banks*, Palgrave
Macmillan Studies in Banking and Financial Institutions,
https://doi.org/10.1007/978-3-030-22426-4